Endorsements for *Re*...

Years ago, I heard Dr. Lester Sumrall say that, sadly, too many Christians live and die in their initial revelation of God. In other words, they never progress very far beyond the door where they came in. I encourage you to accept the challenge issued by Dr. Bill Means to dare to press deeper into kingdom realities and to begin to experience the *Realms Beyond the Gate*!

— Dr. Jefferson K. Thompson
Fresh Water Ministries, International

Dr. Bill Means has brought to the body of Christ an in-depth and very informative book that will take you beyond the gate of salvation into the depths of the principles of the kingdom of God.

Many years of intensive study have brought this book to fruition. I am greatly excited for the body of Christ to receive such great godly wisdom from God's Word and through Dr. Bill Means.

God bless you as you grow from God's wisdom that has been deposited through Dr. Bill Means.

— Pastor Kenny Smith
Greater Dimensions Ministry

Dr. Means is a teacher, a fellow minister, and a treasured friend. He has the ability to take insight into scripture and bring these concepts to life in a simple and yet profound way for the reader. It is extremely impressive as he takes the deep things of God and makes them practical. Enjoy the journey!

— Preston Smith
Lead Pastor, The Bridge Church, Fort Smith

Dr. Bill Means' book is a "How-To" read, revealing how to access the wisdom and authority that's available for every believer who is willing to take the journey to the *Realms Beyond the Gate*.

— Joe Jackson
Evangelist/NFL Retired

REALMS
BEYOND
THE
GATE

7 Principles that Govern God's Kingdom

DR. BILL MEANS

LWP
LIFEWORD PUBLISHING

Realms Beyond the gate: Seven Principles that Govern God's Kingdom

LifeWord Publishing
Post Office Box 201
Pipersville, PA 18947 USA

All Scripture quotations are taken from the King James Version, which is in public domain.

Printed in the United States of America

ISBN: 978-1-7363911-0-5 (Print)

        978-1-7363911-1-2 (E-book)

CONTENTS

FOREWORD

I magine sitting on a couch with Jesus as He reveals the hidden secrets of His Word. That's how I describe Dr. Bill Means' book, *Realms Beyond the Gate*. His scholarly presentation of the covenants reveals the spiritual benefits waiting for those willing to journey from glory to glory. Heaven is our destination, but heaven on earth is our inheritance. Many Christians never venture beyond their salvation experience. I've always said that getting saved is the easy part; working out your salvation demands commitment.

Realms Beyond the Gate explores seven principles that will enlighten, inspire, and empower readers to live as Jesus lived during His earthly walk. Hosea 4:6 (KJV) proclaims, "My people are destroyed for lack of knowledge." God wants people to know *who* He is and *what* He has provided. You are the student, and Jesus is the teacher. As you explore the benefits that accompany your salvation, invite the Holy Spirit to open the windows of your heart and mind.

There is a seat waiting for you next to Jesus. Just as He spoke into the lives of Peter, James, and John, He is ready to invest in you. There is so much more available! If you are tired of just getting by, then my encouragement is to take the journey to *Realms Beyond the Gate*.

— Dr. G. Craig Lauterbach
President/CEO LifeWord Publishing

INTRODUCTION

There are realms of the kingdom of God that most believers never gain access to. This can be because they either don't realize that they exist, or they don't press into the deeper things of God after salvation, therefore, they cannot arrive in these amazing realms.

But the great news is that these "hidden" realms are available to every Christian—and you can access them now! Through this book, my goal is to help you realize what these realms are and show you how you can walk into them and experience the fullness that God intended for you.

In John's letter to the seven churches, known to us as the Book of Revelation, he begins: "I John, who also am your brother, and companion in tribulation, and in the kingdom and patience of Jesus Christ" (Rev. 1:9).

First he identifies himself as "brother" and "companion in tribulation." Then he locates himself "in the kingdom and patience of Jesus Christ."

This should be our goal in this study of the Word: not only to live in the kingdom of God, but in the patience of Jesus Christ. Note that he says he is in the kingdom first and then that he is in the patience of Jesus Christ.

We will begin our study with the kingdom and then end our study with the patience of Jesus Christ. I believe that the first two of the seven principles of the kingdom of God: *blood covenant* and *hesed*—God's faithful unconditional love, will really bring light to this study.

Jesus said, "Seek ye first the kingdom of God, and His righteousness" (Matt. 6:33).

So where is the kingdom? Let's look at what Jesus said in Luke 17:21:

> Neither shall they say, Lo here! or, lo there! for, behold, the kingdom of God is within you.

Jesus had a lot to say about the kingdom.[1]

Throughout the Gospels, Jesus's focus is on the kingdom of God. We need to go back and study these scriptures that deal with the kingdom of God that Jesus talks about, and meditate on these scriptures until we get the revelation of the kingdom of God. We need to be focused on the kingdom of God.

Paul said that if we are born-again children of God, He "hath delivered us from the power of darkness, and hath translated us into the kingdom of his dear Son" (Colossians 1:13). So, like John, that is my location, my address; it is where I live and where I stay. I don't visit the carnal world, coming in and out as I please. I can't live in the kingdom of God and drag one foot over the line. Either I'm in or I'm out; there is no middle ground, period.

Playing to Win

For most of us, the height of our understanding of revelation is that Jesus said if we are born again, the kingdom of God is within us. We know that the Holy Spirit has entered into our spirit, so He is within us. But we don't meditate on that and give it much thought; we just forget about it. The reason that I know that is because if we thought about it, we wouldn't take Him to some of the places we take Him or let Him see some of the things we see.

I guarantee you that if God was sitting on your couch beside you—in the flesh, where you could see Him and talk to Him like He was your best friend—you wouldn't turn on that television. You

---

1. For further study: Matthew 5:3, 20; 7:21; 13:24, 31, 33, 44-45.

wouldn't expose Him to the trash that's on it. But you and I will sit for hours and fill our souls with things of this world that have no value in the kingdom of God.

If you did turn it on, you could watch a baseball game. That's just about the only thing on TV that's not full of trash, except maybe for the commercials.

If we were at my house, I would watch my team. But this year, they are losing. My team makes too many errors. You can't do that and win—you have to have your head in the game. It doesn't matter how good you play your position; if you can't hit the ball, you're going to lose. If you keep losing, there are no postseason games. If there are no postseason games, there is no pennant. If you don't win the pennant, there is no World Series. All you have left is to sit in the stands and watch the winners still playing the game while you sit there thinking about what could have been.

I don't know about you, but I don't want to sit on the sidelines. I want to be in the game. That's what I was created for. I don't want to play with the minor leagues anymore; I want to play in the big leagues. I can do it, but it takes focus and a lot of hard work and dedication.

Brothers and sisters, we have got to be in this game to win. We're not created to be losers. You can have one of three attitudes when playing a game: you can play to win, you can play to draw (tie), or you can play to lose. Never play to lose—that's dishonest, and no one wants to be a loser. I don't ever want to play to draw or tie; that's no fun at all. We should always play to win! The greatest athletes are laser-focused on winning. That should be our attitude, as well. If we have that attitude and are determined to listen closely to our coach—the Holy Spirit—and follow all His instructions, we will be winners. We can be in the lineup of the greatest World Series or Super Bowl the world has ever seen.

Know Where You Are Going

Many Christians don't have a clue who they are. We don't hear preaching or teaching about who we are in Christ anymore. "In Christ realities" are not taught anymore. Instead, it's all about money. "Gimme, gimme, gimme"—that's just about all I've heard in the last ten years. Preachers tell you that you're going to get rich or you're going to the next level if you give them money. I heard a preacher say from the pulpit one day, "God said that the next person that gives me $200 is going to be promoted to their next level." All of a sudden people in the audience were up there giving the preacher checks.

God is not for sale, and you can't buy your next level. Try doing that with a pilot's license, law license, or medical license. They will look at you like you've lost your mind!

We have to get our motivation right and set goals so we know where we are going. Consider the story of Alice in *Alice's Adventures in Wonderland*. In one chapter, Alice is standing in a fork in the road, trying to figure out which way to go. While she is standing there, she notices the Cheshire Cat sitting in a tree nearby.

> "Cheshire Puss," she began . . . . "Would you tell me, please, which way I ought to go from here?"
>
> "That depends a good deal on where you want to get to," said the Cat.
>
> "I don't much care where—" said Alice.
>
> "Then it doesn't matter which way you go," said the Cat.[2]

The same is true for us: if we don't know where we are going, it doesn't much matter which road we take. Our goal and our focus need to be on the kingdom of God.

2. Lewis Carroll, *Alice's Adventures in Wonderland*, (Macmillan: New York, 1865).

Know Who You Are

The reason we don't picture ourselves in the kingdom of God is because we don't know who we are in Christ Jesus.

I am going to give you one example that the Holy Spirit walked me through to help me begin to understand who I am in Christ. Some religious folks will reject this, but it is true nevertheless.

> And God said, Let us make man in our image, after our likeness: and let them have dominion over the fish of the sea, and over the fowl of the air, and over the cattle, and over all the earth, and over every creeping thing that creepeth upon the earth. (Gen. 1:26)

The Lord took me to this scripture and told me to read it and meditate on it. Then after a while, He asked me what this scripture said. I told Him that it said that He made man in His image and likeness and gave him dominion over the whole earth and everything in it.

He asked me, "Who did this?"

"You did it," I answered.

He said "That is right; I am God. But I have many facets of My being, and each facet has a name, so which facet did this, and what is His name?"This led me to study and meditation, because I thought this might be a trick question. After all, God is God, right? Wrong. God has many names, and each name describes a character of God. We have to know which part of His character He is talking about.

I went back to the scripture and reread it in Hebrew, and it said that *Elohim* had said it. So I said to Him that *Elohim* had done it. He said, "That's right." *Elohim* made you in the image and likeness of Himself. Now He's made it personal.

Then He said, "Who is Elohim?"

"He is the God who calls things that are not as though they were; He is the creator God," I said.

He said, "That's right. I made you like Me."

I admit that I had to think about that. He was telling me that I have the power to create and I have dominion. But I knew that there must be other scriptures that would bear that out, so I began to look. This is what I found: What is man, that thou art mindful of him? and the son of man, that thou visitest him? For thou hast made him a little lower than the angels, and hast crowned him with glory and honor. Thou madest him to have dominion over the works of thy hands; thou hast put all things under his feet (Psalm 8:4–6).

These scriptures bear out what God said in Genesis. There's just one problem: it says we are lower than angels. Scripture contradicts that. The Apostle Paul tells us that "we shall judge angels," so we can't be lower than angels (see 1 Corinthians 6:3).

The word *angels* in this scripture is translated from the word *Elohim*. We know that *Elohim* is the creator God. He is not an angel. I don't know why it is translated "angels," but I believe the translators just didn't have the courage to translate it correctly. *Elohim* is used 2,601 times in the Old Testament, and this is the only place that it is translated "angels."[3]

Jesus confirms our lofty status in John 10:34, saying, "Is it not written in your law, 'I said, Ye are gods'?"

In the Greek there is only one word for "god": *theos*. Jesus is quoting Psalm 82:6: "I have said, Ye are gods, and all of you are sons of the Most High."

The bottom line is that we are children of the Most High God, created in the image and likeness of *Elohim*. We have the power to create and

---

3. "H430 - 'ĕlōhîm - Strong's Hebrew Lexicon (ESV)." Blue Letter Bible. Accessed 15 Feb, 2021. https://www.blueletterbible.org//lang/lexicon/lexicon.cfm?Strongs=H430&t=ESV

have dominion because we have His DNA. If you can't accept that, just hang on; when we learn about blood covenant you will be able to see it.

Realms of God

So this is the question: Are we going to get over into the kingdom of God and stay there, walking in the realms of God, or are we going to stay in the carnal world and stay on the sidelines? I suggest that we go after the realms of God.

These realms of God are available to those who are active participants in a blood covenant with Almighty God. They are found only within the kingdom of God. These realms are not available to everyone—only the children of the covenant. The following is a list of just some of the realms that are available to you if you will pay the price necessary to find them:

- Realms of Wisdom
- Realms of Provision
- Realms of Knowledge
- Realms of the Prophetic
- Realms of Understanding
- Realms of Worship
- Realms of Healing
- Realms of Praise
- Realms of Anointing
- Realms of His Presence
- Realms of Faith
- Realms of Miracles

There are seven principles that the Lord has revealed to me that govern the kingdom of God. These seven principles are not all-inclusive. Each has its own sub-principles, which we will not discuss in this book. It would be too exhaustive to try to cover the entire government of the kingdom of God in one book. I am introducing you to the seven basic principles which the Lord revealed to me. You then should be as good Bereans and extend this study for yourself, seeking the leading of the Holy Spirit to reveal even more of the kingdom of God to you (see Acts 17:11).

These seven principles are as follows:

- Blood Covenant
- *Hesed*
- Salvation
- Imputed Righteousness
- Baptism in the Holy Spirit
- Sowing and Reaping
- The Patience of Jesus Christ

In this study, we will break each one of these principles down in detail with the goal of not only receiving the revelation of these principles, but also walking continuously in the realms of God that are found only in the kingdom of God.

Chapter 1: The Journey Begins

A Love Seat

Shew me thy ways, O Lord; teach me thy paths.
(Psalm 25:4)

D
r. A. R. Bernard said, "Everything God does is according to a pattern and based on a principle." He has established principles that govern His creation, and it is to the level that you know and apply these principles that you have any confidence in the consequences of your decisions.

We have established that there are great and wonderful realms of God that we can access. We also understand that these realms are all within the kingdom of God. In Matthew 7:13-14, Jesus instructed us that we must enter into the kingdom of heaven through "the strait gate."

Jesus said in Matthew 6:33, "Seek ye first the kingdom of God and His righteousness." We have to get it into our head and heart that Jesus said what He meant, and meant what He said. He said *first* seek the kingdom and His righteousness.

If we are going to seriously seek after these realms of God, then we must discover the platform—or source—from which everything flows. We must have wisdom and knowledge before we can advance toward our goal. Otherwise, we are like Paul's example: "I therefore so run, not as uncertainly; so fight I, not as one that beateth the air" (1 Corinthians 9:26). If all we are doing is beating the air (shadowboxing), then we are nothing more than pretenders trying to appear as ministers of the gospel.

So how are we going to discover that platform, or source, from which everything will flow? We must have wisdom and knowledge before we can advance toward our goal. Where do we start? We start where Adam, Enoch, Noah, Abraham, Isaac, Jacob, Moses, David, Solomon, Elijah, Elisha, Isaiah, and Jeremiah started. And don't forget about Deborah, a great judge in Israel. Then go to the New Testament and read about Cornelius. We have to go to the source! David said in the Psalms that "the secret of the LORD is with them that fear him; and he will shew them his covenant" (Psalm 25:14).

If the Lord has a secret, I want to know what it is! Let's look back to the Hebrew to see what is actually being said in this scripture. This word *secret* here is the Hebrew word *sôd*, which means: "council (of familiar conversation); divan, circle (of familiar friends); secret counsel; familiar converse, intimacy (with God); to found, fix, establish, lay foundation; to fix or seat themselves close together, sit in conclave; to be founded; to establish, appoint, ordain."[4]

I envision something like an old Victorian loveseat—just room enough for two to sit on it. He has invited me to come to this divan and sit with Him and receive His secret council. And in these times of secret and intimate council, He expounds to me the ways of the kingdom and how I should walk in it.

This is also where He lays His hand on me and imparts to me gifts and anointings. Then He sends me forth in His name and in His power to accomplish the assignments He has given me.

But I must first qualify to sit on that couch with Him—I must "fear the Lord." What does that mean? The Strong's concordance defines it as, "fearing; morally, reverent:--afraid, fear (-ful)."[5] A better definition

4. Brown-Driver-Briggs' Hebrew Definitions, s.v. *sôd*, 1906, public domain.
5. Strong's Hebrew and Greek Dictionaries, s.v. *"perisseuo,"* 1890, public domain.

in this context would be "a high level of respect." This is the problem with the English language—it just does not translate well from the Hebrew and Greek.

We will use the rule of interpretation to get an understanding of what is being said here. The rule is, "You interpret scripture with scripture." So the question is: Who qualifies to sit on this couch? We will look at Psalms 15 and 24 to get the answer.

> Lord, who shall abide in thy tabernacle? who shall dwell in thy holy hill? He that walketh uprightly, and worketh righteousness, and speaketh the truth in his heart. He that backbiteth not with his tongue, nor doeth evil to his neighbour, nor taketh up a reproach against his neighbor. In whose eyes a vile person is contemned; but he honoureth them that fear the LORD. He that sweareth to his own hurt, and changeth not. He that putteth not out his money to usury, nor taketh reward against the innocent. He that doeth these things shall never be moved. (Ps. 15)

> Who shall ascend into the hill of the LORD? or who shall stand in his holy place? He that hath clean hands, and a pure heart; who hath not lifted up his soul unto vanity, nor sworn deceitfully. (Ps. 24:3–4)

The secret of the Lord is with them who highly honor Him and faithfully obey His commands.

Now let's look at the word *shew* from Psalm 25:14. It comes from the Hebrew *yada`*, which means: "to know, to reveal, to demonstrate; to know, learn to know; to perceive and see, find out and discern; to know by experience; to know how, be skillful in; to have knowledge, be wise; to be made known, be or become known; be revealed, to be instructed." Some scholars believe verse 14 should be translated, "And His covenant is to make them to know."

Leave the Past Behind

Let us look a little deeper and see how God works with us.

> Good and upright is the LORD: therefore will he teach
> sinners in the way. The meek will he guide in judgment:
> and the meek will he teach his way. (Ps. 25:8–9)

So the sinner He *leads* in the way, and the meek He *teaches* His way.
God does not treat everyone the same way.

> All the paths of the LORD are mercy and truth unto such
> as keep his covenant and his testimonies. . . . What man
> is he that feareth the LORD? him shall he teach in the way
> that he shall choose. . . .

> The secret of the LORD is with them that fear him; and
> [His covenant is to make them know]. (Ps. 25:10,12,14)

Brothers and Sisters, it is all in all, or not at all—this is the requirement
of true devotion.

I am a blessed man and God keeps reminding me of this scripture:
"For unto whomsoever much is given, of him shall be much required"
(Luke 12:48). We are held accountable for our knowledge.

These verses speak entirely about relationships; they say nothing
about works. Yes, works come out of this relationship—but without a
relationship, there are no meaningful works.

Let's go back to Matthew 6:33: "Seek ye first the kingdom of God
and His righteousness." First things first—we must know and have
intimate knowledge of the King and His kingdom.

This must be our goal, our passion. We may not be there yet, but we
must aspire to achieve that goal. As Paul said to the Philippians:

CHAPTER 1: THE JOURNEY BEGINS

> Not as though I had already attained, either were already perfect: but I follow after, if that I may apprehend that for which also I am apprehended of Christ Jesus. Brethren, I count not myself to have apprehended: but this one thing I do, forgetting those things which are behind, and reaching forth unto those things which are before, I press toward the mark for the prize of the high calling of God in Christ Jesus. (Phil. 3:12–14)

This is not the end goal; this is where I begin. This is the platform or source that we must discover from which everything must flow. We must press toward the mark for the prize of the high calling of God in Christ Jesus. We need to learn from Paul's example, "forgetting those things that are behind, and reaching forth unto those things which are before."

Paul was guilty of trying to destroy the church. He wasn't just someone who talked against the church. He didn't just persecute them; he arrested the people and put them in jail—and some he killed. Paul had discovered that he couldn't move forward if he lived in that past. He had to put it away.

When Paul accepted the call of God, he had to repent of his past sins. He had to walk away from all the evil that he was guilty of. If Paul was going to be useful in the kingdom of God, he would have to not only receive God's forgiveness, but to forgive himself.

Paul said *forgetting* what is behind. *Forgetting* is translated from the Greek word *epilanthanomai* (ep-ee-lan-than'-om-ahee). It means to "lose out of mind; to neglect or to forget."[6] We have to put our past behind us forever. We can't change it; it's history. You can't change history. It is what it is. So you must put it away. You must repent of your sins, forgive yourself, accept God's forgiveness, and walk away from it. That's what Paul did. He knew that he couldn't live in his past and move forward, so he forgave himself and walked away from it.

---

6. Thayer and Smith, "Greek Lexicon entry for *Epilanthanomai*, The KJV New Testament Greek Lexicon, Bible Study Tools online, accessed October 26, 2020, https://www.biblestudytools.com/lexicons/greek/kjv/epilanthanomai.html.

That's why we are reminded in Scripture:

> As far as the east is from the west, so far hath he removed our transgressions from us (Psalm 103:12).And Jesus said unto him, No man, having put his hand to the plough, and looking back, is fit for the kingdom of God. (Luke 9:62)

Things were never easy for Paul. Reading the book of Acts, you would think that Paul immediately began preaching the gospel after his encounter with Jesus, but that's not what happened. The disciples were afraid of him and would not accept him. The Jews wanted to kill him, so he had to run for his life. Paul went home to Tarsus and was on the backside of the desert for fourteen years, where he was being trained by Jesus.

Here's something to think about. Jesus trained the disciples for three years, but He took fourteen years to train Paul. Paul was not a slow learner; he was the brightest student Gamaliel had in his university in Jerusalem. Compare Paul's ministry to the others.

The more time God takes to develop you in your ministry, the greater the ministry will be. You must be patient and wait on God. This waiting time is a great opportunity to stay before God and be taught of the Holy Spirit. The worst thing you can do is compare yourself to others. They have their calling; you have yours. When you're ready to go to the front lines as a faithful soldier, nothing and no one will be able to stop you.

Also, notice that when God was ready to begin to use Paul, He sent Barnabas to get him. Paul served under Barnabas before he was on his own.

Passing the Test

Jesus said, "And if ye have not been faithful in that which is another man's, who shall give you that which is your own?" (Luke 16:12).

CHAPTER 1: THE JOURNEY BEGINS

Many ministers resist or even try to skip this step in their preparation for their ministry. If you do, it may appear that you are having some success, but I assure you that it will be limited. God doesn't take shortcuts. You are not going to fulfill the call on your life without passing this test. You don't move up without passing the test that God sets before you. I don't care how many awesome prophecies you get; it's not going to come to pass until you do it God's way. It is God's will, God's way, and God's timing.

Until you have passed this test, you have not fully surrendered your life to God. You are still making your own decisions, directing your own path, and deciding your own destiny. This is very hard for a lot of men and women in ministry. Remember that Jesus said, "Many are called but few are chosen" (Matthew 22:14).

There is a huge difference between being called and being chosen. Sooner or later, you will figure this out. The question is: How many years are you going to lose before you are ready to surrender your life to God? Paul had to learn it, the disciples had to learn it, and you and I have to learn it. God can't trust you until you have been tested.

Until you have been toughened by these tests that God walks you through, you will never be able to stand. If you have any success in the kingdom of God, there will be an all-out assault on you, your ministry, and your family. If you have not been toughened and prepared and fully equipped, you will tuck tail and run.

I like to use the analogy of Navy Seal Training. It is the most rigorous, stressful, agonizing, painful experience a man could go through. That in itself is bad enough, only the toughest men will complete the test. What makes it tough is that on the beach where they are training, there is a bell mounted on a pole, and all they have to do to stop the pain is ring the bell. Those who ring that bell were called, but they will not be chosen.

Those of us who have rung that bell are not discarded. It just means that we were not ready. We have to go back and do it again. Jesus doesn't quit on us. The only ones who lose are the ones who quit and don't get back up when they are knocked down. We have to go back and do it His way. We have to complete the steps as He sets them before us.

There is nothing easy about the ministry. Jesus Christ gave His life for you; are you willing to fully give your life for Him?

Our primary goal is to get on that couch and develop a close intimate relationship with the Holy Spirit. Out of that relationship flows everything that we will need to successfully fulfill the call that is on our life. He wants you first. Then the call follows. Remember: first things first.

Getting through the Gate

Now that we have some idea of where we want to go, we have to take the first step to enter into the kingdom of God.

> Jesus answered and said unto him, Verily, verily, I say unto thee, Except a man be born again, he cannot see the kingdom of God. . . . Verily, verily, I say unto thee, Except a man be born of water and of the Spirit, he cannot enter into the kingdom of God. That which is born of the flesh is flesh; and that which is born of the Spirit is spirit. (John 3:3, 5–6)

Jesus makes it clear: you must be born again before you can enter into the kingdom of God. But how do we enter the kingdom?

> Enter ye in at the strait gate: for wide is the gate, and broad is the way, that leadeth to destruction, and many there be which go in thereat: Because strait is the gate, and narrow is the way, which leadeth unto life, and few there be that find it. (Matt. 7:13–14)

It is interesting that Jesus used the phrase "strait gate." *Strait* is translated from the Greek word *stenos*. A strait place is a hard place. It can also be defined as a dangerous place. Many people when they see this scripture are instantly reminded of the old saying, "We must walk the straight and narrow path." However, notice the difference in the spelling of the two words. *Strait*, as I said, is a hard and dangerous place. *Straight* signifies a direction, such as a straight line between points A and B. They are two completely different words.

Jesus was familiar with the word *strait*. According to traditional history, as a young man, Jesus occasionally accompanied His mother's uncle, Joseph of Arimathaea, when he went to what we call today the British Isles to check on his lead mines. Joseph was one of the richest men in Israel. They traveled by ship and had to sail the Mediterranean Sea through the Straits of Gibraltar.

The straits are a very dangerous place for a ship. Just under the water are great boulders that can't be seen from the ship. If the ship hits one of these boulders, it would knock a hole in the bottom. The ship would sink and the freight would be lost, as well as some of the sailors.

Therefore, the ship's captain would sail the ship to the entrance of the straits and put out the anchor. He would wait for a pilot to get into a rowboat and row out to the ship and come aboard. The pilot knew the waters and the safe path through the straits and would guide the ship safely to the other side of the straits. Then the pilot would get back into his rowboat and go to the shore and wait for a ship coming from the other direction.

Jesus knew that getting through that strait gate was not going to be easy. When He said to enter in through the strait gate, He knew that there would be few that could do it. In Luke, He made an even stronger statement.

> Then said one unto him, Lord, are there few that be saved? And he said unto them, "Strive to enter in at the strait gate: for many, I say unto you, will seek to enter in, and shall not be able." (Luke 13:23–24)

Apparently, Jesus had said something that made them think that not very many would be able to enter the kingdom of God, because they asked Him about how many would make it. To put it in my words, I think what Jesus said to them was, "That's right; you are going to have to strive to enter the strait gate."

Look at the word *strive*. It is translated from the Greek word *agōnizomai* (ag-o-nid'-zom-ahee). It means "to *struggle*, literally (to *compete* for a prize), figuratively (to *contend* with an adversary), or generally (to *endeavor* to accomplish something): fight, labor fervently, strive." It is where we get our English word *agony*. [7]

Using these words, Jesus is telling us this salvation thing is not easy to obtain. He says we must endeavor, contend, and struggle to the point of agony. Jesus went on to say that there are going to be a lot of people who try to enter in, but just can't make it.

Jesus also said in Matthew 7:14 that we not only have to go through a strait gate, but we also must go through a "narrow way." The word *narrow* comes from the Greek word *thlibo* (pronounced thlee'bo), meaning "to *crowd* (literally or figuratively): afflict, narrow, throng, suffer tribulation, trouble."[8] Thayer defines it as "to press (as grapes), press hard upon; a compressed way; narrow straitened, contracted; metaphorically to trouble, afflict, distress."[9] The Greek word for *way* here is *hodos*: "a *road*; by implication a *progress* (the route, act or distance); figuratively a *mode* or *means:* journey, (high-) way." [10]

Jesus is telling us that we are not only going to have to strive to get through the strait gate, but we are also going to have to travel a narrow way, which is also suffering tribulation and trouble. Let us look at what else Jesus said when addressing this question of how many would make it through the gate into the kingdom of God.

7. Strong's Hebrew and Greek Dictionaries, s.v. "*agōnizomai,*" 1890, public domain.

8. Strong's Hebrew and Greek Dictionaries, s.v. "*thlibo,*" 1890, public domain.

9. Thayer and Smith, "Greek Lexicon entry for Thlibo," "The KJV New Testament Greek Lexicon," accessed November 11, 2020, https://www.biblestudytools.com/lexicons/greek/kjv/thlibo.html.

10. Strong's Hebrew and Greek Dictionaries, s.v. "*hodos,*" 1890, public domain.

When once the master of the house is risen up, and hath shut to the door, and ye begin to stand without, and to knock at the door, saying, Lord, Lord, open unto us; and he shall answer and say unto you, I know you not whence ye are: Then shall ye begin to say, We have eaten and drunk in thy presence, and thou hast taught in our streets. But he shall say, I tell you, I know you not whence ye are; depart from me, all ye workers of iniquity. There shall be weeping and gnashing of teeth, when ye shall see Abraham, and Isaac, and Jacob, and all the prophets, in the kingdom of God, and you yourselves thrust out. And they shall come from the east, and from the west, and from the north, and from the south, and shall sit down in the kingdom of God. And, behold, there are last which shall be first, and there are first which shall be last. (Luke 13:25–30)

Brothers and sisters, it's not a simple matter to get into the kingdom of God. They said all you have to do is walk the aisle, shake the preacher's hand, and say a prayer after him. They dunk you in their tank, you join the church, and that's it. You are saved from now on no matter what you do. Once saved, always saved.

I wish it were that easy. If you don't want to accept this, go back and read the scripture again. Jesus lays it out. You must be born again; otherwise, you are not going in. Only a few will find it.

Not everyone that saith unto me, Lord, Lord, shall enter into the kingdom of heaven; but he that doeth the will of my Father which is in heaven. Many will say to me in that day, Lord, Lord, have we not prophesied in thy name? and in thy name have cast out devils? and in thy name done many wonderful works? And then will I profess unto them, I never knew you: depart from me, ye that work iniquity. (Matt. 7:21–23)

Remember, this is a red-letter King James; Jesus is talking. He says that everyone who professes to be His is not really His. These people are saying that they are ministers of the gospel. They are prophesying, casting out devils, and doing miracles. Jesus is saying just because you do that, it doesn't make you His. Your heart is not with Him. He says He doesn't know them. That word *know* means that He has no relationship with them.

Jesus makes it clear that "only those that obey the Father will enter the kingdom of God." We must not be fooled by religious works. We must work as the Spirit wills, not as we will.

When the drawing comes, and we respond and have a true born-again experience, our spirit comes alive. The Holy Spirit enters into our spirit, and He becomes the pilot of our lives, leading us right through that strait gate and narrow way into the kingdom of God.

Look at what Matthew Henry had to say about this over three hundred years ago.

> 1. A quickening exhortation and direction: *Strive to enter in at the strait gate.* This is directed not to him only that asked the question, but to all, to us, it is in the plural number: *Strive ye.* Note, (1.) All that will be saved must *enter in at the strait gate,* must undergo a change of the whole man, such as amounts to no less than being born again, and must submit to a strict discipline.

> 2. Those that would enter in at the strait gate must *strive to enter.* It is a hard matter to get to heaven and a point that will not be gained without a great deal of care and pains, of difficulty and diligence. We must strive with God in prayer, wrestle as Jacob, strive against sin and satan. We must strive in every duty of religion; strive with our own

hearts, *agōnizesthe* - "*Be in an agony;* strive as those that run for a prize; excite and exert ourselves to the utmost."[11]

The great preacher Charles Finney once remarked that most people who attend church are probably not born again. When asked why he believed this, Finney was said to have remarked that "it was impossible for true children of God to live in blatant sin as many believers do." Finney made this statement over a hundred years ago.

As I contemplate the amount of sin that is so prevalent in the church today, it makes me wonder: how many people who attend church in our day are not genuinely born again?

Paul says that once we are born again, we are to walk in righteousness and holiness. Today you cannot tell the church from the world. Sin is rampant in the church today.

Jesus told the church at Pergamum:

> But I have a few things against thee, because thou hast there them that hold the doctrine of Balaam, who taught Balac to cast a stumblingblock before the children of Israel, to eat things sacrificed unto idols, and to commit fornication. So hast thou also them that hold the doctrine of the Nicolaitans, which thing I hate. (Rev. 2:14–15)

Jesus was not pleased with the church at Pergamum. These church members were practicing the doctrine of the Nicolaitans. Jesus said He hated that doctrine. It was the teaching that you could live like the world and still be saved. They practiced fornication with no sense of guilt at all. This was a very corrupt church.

The so-called Christian churches in twenty-first century America are just like them. How many people do you know who are sitting on the

---

11. Matthew Henry, *Matthew Henry's Commentary on the Whole Bible*, (1708 – 1714), Public Domain.

church pew and living with someone that they are not married to? It's not unusual at all.

I was talking to a man one day who was on the praise team of one of the very large churches in the region. The church was fortunate enough that they had three praise teams. Therefore they could rotate and not have to do it every Sunday. He was telling me that one Sunday morning how he and another man were on the platform getting ready for the service to start when the other fellow began to tell him how the church was full of beautiful women. He then began to point out all the women he had affairs with in the church. He said some of the women were single and some of them were married. He said that it was no problem getting all the sex you wanted in that church.

Brothers and sisters, this is not the church that Jesus is coming for! Jesus set the standards much higher—and will not tolerate open sin. I beseech you therefore, brethren, by the mercies of God, that ye present your bodies a living sacrifice, holy, acceptable unto God, which is your reasonable service (Romans 12:1).

> According as he hath chosen us in him before the foundation of the world, that we should be holy and without blame before him in love. (Eph. 1:4)

> That he might present it to himself a glorious church, not having spot, or wrinkle, or any such thing; but that it should be holy and without blemish. (Eph. 5:27)

You cannot live in sin and die in Christ!

Brothers and sisters, we need to stop before we go any further and ask ourselves, "Are we born again?" Did we just have an emotional experience, or did we truly become a new creature in Christ? This is very important—if we are not born again, we are not in covenant with Jesus, and we are not going to spend eternity with Him when we die. This is between you and the Lord, but you must make certain of it.

Now we are through the gate. This is a problem for many saints. They get through the gate and sit down. They have been told that that is all there is. But it's not all there is; it is only the beginning. God has provided much more for us. Once we get through the gate, we don't sit down; this is when we must begin to seek.

Drawing, Striving, and Seeking

First, there is a drawing: "No man can come to me, except the Father which hath sent me draw him: and I will raise him up at the last day" (John 6:44).

Second, there is a striving: "Strive to enter in at the strait gate: for many, I say unto you, will seek to enter in, and shall not be able" (Luke 13:24).

Third, there is a seeking: "But seek ye first the kingdom of God, and his righteousness; and all these things shall be added unto you" (Matt. 6:33).

If you're not entering the kingdom of God to do the King's business, you're not going in. A person who has a true born-again experience submits their entire life to God. He's not selling timeshare condos. You can't just go in and out as you please. When you go in, you don't come out, nor do you *want* to come out.

This is how you live now—you go after the things of the kingdom: "Ask, and it shall be given you; seek, and ye shall find; knock, and it shall be opened unto you: For everyone that asketh receiveth; and he that seeketh findeth; and to him that knocketh it shall be opened" (Matt. 7:7–8). This asking, seeking, and knocking is a lifestyle we now live. It never ends. We continually seek more of the kingdom, and we do that by seeking more of the King.

We have been sealed with the Holy Spirit. He lives within us. Jesus said, "The kingdom of God cometh not with observation: Neither shall they say, Lo here! or, lo there! for, behold, the kingdom of God is within you" (Luke 17:20–21).

Now that we have positioned ourselves and have an understanding of some things, we can continue.

The realms of the kingdom are beyond the gate. Therefore, we have to go through the gate before we can access them. Now that we have done so, we will study the realms of the kingdom which are seven major principles that the Holy Spirit has taught me that govern the kingdom of God.

CHAPTER 2: THE LANGUAGE OF COVENANT

W e Christians believe that the Bible is the inspired Word of God given to us by the Holy Spirit through revelations given to holy men of God. We understand the Bible to be a book of the covenant. The Old Testament and the New Testament are translated from the word *covenant*. So they are, in other words, the old covenant and the new covenant.

We further believe that the Bible is God's instruction manual to His people. We believe that God intends for us to study this manual, and in doing so, we will know and obey His commandments, thereby living a proper life on the earth and receive eternal life with Jesus when we die.

I believe that most Christians with a pure heart toward God make every effort to walk upright before God and live a godly life. Knowing that we still sin from time to time, we have an advocate with the Father and can be forgiven if we truly repent from the heart.

I also believe that most Christians, including the fivefold ministry, have very little understanding of the "biblical covenant," as to its origin, intent, application, and effect. I am not saying that we don't know anything, but I am suggesting that because we don't know and understand covenant language, along with ancient rites and customs, we may not be aware of the exceptional power and privilege of the covenant.

The twenty-first century American Christian has no personal experience or understanding of blood covenant. Never have I heard of a meeting being called to establish a blood covenant between two men where their families and friends come together to witness the two men drinking each other's blood or cutting their hands and putting them together so that the blood would intermingle and they would become "blood brothers." I most certainly have never heard of a wife and her children hiring an assassin to kill her husband because he had broken a covenant and disgraced the family. God said that when a man breaks a covenant that even the ground he walks on is cursed (see Genesis 3:17).

The closest we come to experiencing a covenant is in a wedding ceremony. The problem is that twenty minutes after the ceremony the bride and groom can't tell you what the vows were that they swore before God.

The Holy Spirit led me into the study of the blood covenant over twenty years ago. I read several books on the subject written by notable authors and learned much about covenant. However, I noticed that the older the book, the more I began to understand covenant language. As I would read these ancient books I would be reminded of phrases in the Bible that used the same words that were written in these books. This began to open the Bible to me, giving me the ability to see covenant in the Bible where I had never seen it before. The more I learned about the language of the covenant, the more the Bible began to come alive for me, and the more I began to truly understand what this blood covenant really is, and the power and privilege it carries.

For me, this has been a journey of learning and discovery led by the Holy Spirit in the study of biblical blood covenant. The Holy Spirit led me to not just read, but study the writings of great men of God.

The first obstacle that must be overcome in any study of the Word of God is to understand that the Bible was written by Eastern people, to Eastern people, in Eastern language. We cannot translate language that is thousands of years old to our twenty-first century English language and expect to retain the full meaning of the idea behind the word being translated. Therefore, if we want to know more about what is being said, we have to dig deeper than Strong's or Thayer's.

Webster defines the word *covenant* as:

> A mutual agreement, or a stipulation in such an agreement; the promises of God as revealed in the Scriptures, conditioned on man's obedience, repentance, and faith, etc.; a contract in writing and under seal, or the document or writing containing the terms of agreement; a form of action for the violating of a promise or contract under deal.[12]

Even this detailed description of the word doesn't fully embrace the whole idea behind it. If you take a look at covenants throughout the ages, even dating back to ancient times, we find that covenants were sacred promises that were made by each party's blood making contact with each other or even by consuming the blood of the other party—as a picture of the life of each being brought together and was now inseparable in that union.

The root of the Hebrew word *bereeth* (covenant) means "to cut, to fetter, to bind together, to fix, to establish, to pour out, to eat, and to cut where blood flows."[13] It is easy to see how these words may have been taken as referring to the one primitive idea of an established union.

The blood covenant was first established by God in the garden of Eden. The Bible speaks of a covenant between God and Noah, Abraham, Isaac, and Jacob, then Moses and Joshua. The word *beriyth* is used 284 times in the Old Testament.[14] Here are a few examples:

---

12. Noah Webster, Webster's Collegiate Dictionary, s.v. "covenant," (G. & C. Merriam: Springfield, Mass, 1913), public domain.

13. Strong's Hebrew and Greek Dictionaries, s.v. "*bereeth,*" 1890. Public Domain.

14. Brown, Driver, Briggs and Gesenius, "Hebrew Lexicon entry for B@riyth," "The KJV Old Testament Hebrew Lexicon," accessed November 11, 2020. https://www.biblestudytools.com/lexicons/hebrew/kjv/beriyth.html.

- In 2 Samuel 23:5, David said that he had an everlasting covenant with God.

- In 2 Kings 11:17, Jehoiada renewed the covenant that the children of Israel had with God.

- In 2 Kings 23:3, Josiah reestablished the covenant between himself and the people of Judah and God.

- In 2 Chronicles 13:5, God made a covenant with David with a "covenant of salt."

There are many scriptures throughout the Old Testament that speak of the covenant. As you study the Old Testament you will notice that God judges His people according to how they respond to the covenant. When they honor the covenant, they prosper, and when they turn their back on God and dishonor the covenant, they go into captivity. Didn't God say He never changes? You might want to ask yourself, "How is this working out today for me? Am I honoring God and His covenant?" If you don't know anything about the covenant you have with Almighty God, how can you honor it and be obedient to it? If we are not obedient and honor the covenant, how can we expect God to bless us and give us the promises of the covenant?

The Bible is constantly speaking of the covenant. After reading this book you should go back and read the entire Old Testament and you will see that it is entirely about covenant. Then when you read the New Testament, you will readily see how it is connected to the old covenant and has been made new through Jesus. It is all about covenant! We need to get that perspective.

God sees His covenant like a wedding covenant. Jesus is the Groom and we, the church, are the bride. God holds this covenant as being very sacred and will not tolerate the covenant being broken. As we study covenant we need to retain this idea.

Covenant is Rooted in Honor

The very foundation of covenant is rooted in honor and integrity.

The fifteenth Psalm identifies who is qualified to be in covenant with Almighty God. Let's look at it again:

> Lord, who shall abide in thy tabernacle? Who shall dwell in thy holy hill? He that walketh uprightly, and worketh righteousness, and speaketh the truth in his heart. He that backbiteth not with his tongue, nor doeth evil to his neighbor [friend], nor taketh up a reproach against his neighbor [kin]. In whose eyes a vile person is contemned [despised]: but he honoreth them that fear [revere] the Lord. He that sweareth to his own hurt, and changeth not. He that putteth not out his money to usury, nor taketh reward against the innocent. He that doeth these things shall never be moved.

Those who are qualified are the righteous, the truthful, the just, and the honest. Thomas Jefferson called this psalm the picture of a true gentleman. It describes how we should live. A man's word is his bond. It is sealed with a handshake. When he makes a solemn oath and swears on a Bible, it is held sacred. If you do not walk in honor and integrity, you can never enter into a blood covenant.

Blood and Covenants

Now let's look at some ancient customs and beliefs in regards to blood and covenants.

> For the life of the flesh is in the blood: and I have given it to you upon the altar to make an atonement for your souls: for it is the blood that maketh an atonement for the soul. (Lev. 17:11)

There has been a universal belief throughout all ages and on all continents that life was in the blood. They believed that the heart was the blood source, and the blood not only carried the life of that person or animal but it also carried the very nature of that life. Therefore they believed that if one could take in blood from another that the transfer of the blood would not only transfer the life of that other, but would also transfer the nature of the one whose blood was transferred whether man or animal.

There are ancient customs recorded of men drinking the blood of their first enemy killed in battle thereby acquiring the courage and nature of that enemy. There are also customs of men drinking the blood of their first kill of a deer or other large animal that was considered brave or cunning. The idea being that in drinking the blood they would acquire the nature of the one killed.

The life is in the blood and the nature of that person is in the blood. Therefore when two men cut their hands and put them together so that the blood flows into each other they become one in life and nature. They each acquire the life and nature of the other becoming one with each other. A blood brother is considered a stronger bond than even two brothers of the same mother. There is nothing held back from each other. If one needs anything and the other can supply it, it is immediately offered.

Man in ancient times believed that God is life and all life came from God. Therefore, if blood carries life, then there is a way to become one with their God, hence the blood sacrifice. They believed that by the pouring out of innocent blood on the altar they would become one with their god.

The Bible gives us an example of this in Genesis, where Abel brought the lamb as his sacrifice to God (see Genesis 4:4). It is because of the law of substitution that substitute blood can be offered in order to enter into a covenant with God.

There are ancient customs where the blood of the firstborn son is poured out on the altar to their god in order to come into covenant with their god.

Henry Clay Trumbull had a lot to say about this subject and wrote whole volumes about the blood covenant. Here are some interesting points that he makes:

> Perhaps the most ancient existing form of religious worship, as also the simplest and most primitive form,

is to be found in China, in the state religion, represented by the Emperor's worship at the Temple of Heaven, in Peking. And in that worship, the idea of the worshiper's inter-communion with God, through the body and blood of the sacrificial offering, is disclosed, even if not always recognized, by all the representative Western authorities on the religions of China.

"The Chinese idea of a sacrifice to the supreme [149] spirit of Heaven and of Earth is that of a banquet. There is no trace of any other idea," says Dr. Edkins....

The idea of an approach to God through blood—blood as a means of favor, even if not blood as a canceling of guilt—is obvious, in the outpouring of blood by the Emperor when he approaches God for his worship in the Temple of Heaven. The symbolic sacrifice in that worship, which precedes the communion, is of a whole "burnt offering, of a bullock, entire and without blemish"; and the blood of that offering is reverently poured out into the earth, to be buried there, according to the thought of man and the teachings of God in all the ages. It is even claimed that as early as 2697 B. C., it was the blood of the first-born which must be poured out toward God—as a means of favor—in the Emperor's approach for communion with [151] God; "a first-born male," being offered up "as a whole burnt sacrifice," in this worship....Access to God being attained by the Emperor, the Emperor enjoys communion with God in the Temple of Heaven.[15]

Doesn't this remind you of God requiring Abraham to sacrifice his firstborn son?

15. Henry Clay Trumbull, The Blood Covenant, (John D. Wattles & Co.: Philadelphia, 1898), 148-151, Public Domain.

We have to study the meaning and growth of words in the light of ancient customs and rites and ideas. By doing this we begin to learn covenant language, and in so doing, we then begin to understand how ancient people thought about the power of blood and how they could become one with their god through blood.

The thought and belief were that life is in the blood; therefore, by acquiring another's blood, they can acquire their life and all that is good in them. The obvious next step is that if they can acquire their god's blood, then they can become one with him and be in covenant with him.

We, as born-again Christians, believe we have done just that. We are one with Almighty God through the blood of Jesus Christ.

As we continue our study we will discover just how this was done.

Chapter 3: Ancient Covenant

W hen God created man in the beginning, He placed Adam in the garden of Eden and determined that His relationship with man would be established in and governed by a blood covenant. It was because Adam violated that covenant that sin entered the world. Hosea speaks of this: "But they like men have transgressed the covenant: there have they dealt treacherously against me" (Hosea 6:7). The word *men* in this scripture is translated from the Hebrew word *Adam*.

We see the idea of covenant carried over as mankind began to populate the earth. As soon as Noah left the ark, he built an altar to honor God and God immediately established His covenant with Noah.

> And Noah builded an altar unto the LORD; and took of every clean beast, and of every clean fowl, and offered burnt offerings on the altar....And God blessed Noah and his sons, and said unto them, Be fruitful, and multiply, and replenish the earth...And God spake unto Noah, and to his sons with him, saying, "And I, behold, I establish my covenant with you, and with your seed after you....I do set my bow in the cloud, and it shall be for a token of a covenant between me and the earth." (Gen. 8:20; 9:1, 8–9, 13)

As you can see from scripture, covenants have been in the earth from the beginning of creation. God created the principle of covenant in order to establish an unbreakable bond between man and God. When a covenant was entered into, whether it was between man and God or man and man, it was not to be broken by either party. The law of the covenant stated that the one that broke the covenant had to die. The covenant was established in blood and therefore could be redeemed only by blood. When the covenant is broken the man that broke the covenant was cursed—even the ground that he walked on was cursed (see Gen. 3:17).

The blood covenant was considered the highest contract that could be entered into by man and must be honored at any cost, including the forfeiture of the man's life who broke the covenant. It would so dishonor the family that even the wife and children would hire an assassin to take the life of the man in order to redeem the covenant.

In my research and study, I have found that the blood covenant was in use throughout history. It could be found on every continent and in every culture dating from Noah up into the 19th century. It seems that beginning in the twentieth century it began to fade away—people no longer made blood covenants or honored them if they did. Civilization today is so far removed from the blood covenant that we have no understanding of its weight or sacredness. Blood covenants can still be found in Africa and possibly in other countries, but when I asked African men in Kenya about the sacredness of the blood covenant, they said that if the covenant was broken, they would no longer consider taking the life of the covenant breaker. It would seem to me that if the covenant could not be redeemed by blood, then it wasn't a blood covenant to start with.

In studying the various peoples and cultures where blood covenant was practiced, I found that they all had procedures and rituals that they followed, whether the covenant was between man and man or tribe and tribe. The procedures and rituals varied from one culture to the other, but they all had the same objective, which was to become one with the person or tribe making covenant. In making covenant the law of substitution could be invoked. Praise God for this law because without it,

Jesus could not have been our substitute. The law of substitution simply stated that another person could stand in for the parties making covenant. As their representatives, the blood covenant was just as binding as if the parties themselves had gone through the rituals of cutting covenant.

In the typical procedure, prior to the covenant ritual, the two parties would come together and negotiate the agreement that was to be made between them. The negotiations would be firmly agreed to and written down by both parties. The negotiations consisted of the promises made by each party and also the curses that would come upon the party that broke the covenant, should that happen.

The next step in making the covenant would be to choose the representative for each side if the law of substitution was to be invoked. This man would have to be a man of high integrity and character who is revered by the tribe or the man making covenant.

The covenant site was chosen. It would be a place where all the witnesses could gather around and see clearly the ritual.

The next step in the procedure was the selection of the sacrificial animals. They were most often large animals that would shed a great deal of blood when they were slaughtered. The animals were cut from the back of the neck down the backbone. The two halves fell to the ground, laying opposite of each other. Their blood poured out on the ground between the two halves. This caused a pool of blood that might come up to the ankles of the men as they stepped into what they called the "blood alley."

As the ceremony began, each representative would step into the blood alley, take off their coat, and exchange it with the other representative. The coat represented the strength and authority of each family. By exchanging coats they symbolically exchanged authority. Then they exchanged their weapons belts, which meant that they would fight one another's battles.

In Ephesians 6 where the Bible talks about putting on the whole armor of God, it is making a covenant statement. He has given us His armor and joined forces with us to fight our enemy, the devil.

The men then standing in the blood up to the ankles repeated to the witnesses the agreement made during the negotiation process. Then they began to walk up and down in the blood alley in a figure-eight pattern, which signifies infinity—indicating that this covenant was established for all eternity. They then stood in the middle of the blood alley and stated all the promises and curses of the negotiated covenant.

A biblical example of this part of the ceremony is written in Deuteronomy 28, where God through Moses is stating His covenant conditions to His chosen people in the desert.

The next step in the ceremony was the covenant cut. Each man would cut themselves on the hand or wrist, letting the blood flow, and each raising their hand to show the witnesses the blood running down their arm. They would then put their hands or wrists together where the blood was flowing to allow their blood to mingle with the other. This symbolized that they had become of one blood and were one with each other. At this moment they became blood brothers. The old saying "Blood is thicker than water" is from this practice; the full saying is, "Blood of the covenant is thicker than the water of the womb." It means that blood brothers are closer than natural brothers that came through the water breaking of their natural mother.

With this concluded, the two men or the two tribes have become one man or one tribe. One of the traditions of a covenant of two families would be to exchange names. For instance, if the Smith family and Jones family entered into covenant, at this point in the ceremony they would become the Smith-Jones family. From that day forward that would be their name.

Among the ancients it was common for them to establish a monument in recognition of the covenant made that day. It could be anything from a pile of stones to planting a tree that was known to live many years.

The idea was that anyone looking upon the memorial would remember the covenant and the promises it represents. Abraham made a covenant with Abimelech, and as a memorial, gave him seven ewe lambs (see Gen. 21:22–32).

Consummating the Covenant

The last step in the covenant ceremony was the covenant meal. The two sides came together celebrating their new covenant and consummating it by eating it together. Two elements of the covenant were usually bread and wine. The bread represented the body, and the wine represented the blood. The meal of bread and wine symbolized each family giving themselves to the other family even to the point of dying for one another if need be. They ate "in remembrance" of what they did that day in cutting a covenant together.

Take a look at the following scriptures and realize that we are as much in covenant with Almighty God as though we had cut our right hand and grabbed hold of God's right hand and mingled our blood and became one with the Father.

> Then Jesus said unto them, Verily, verily, I say unto you, Except ye eat the flesh of the Son of man, and drink his blood, ye have no life in you. (John 6:53)

> For my flesh is meat indeed, and my blood is drink indeed. He that eateth my flesh, and drinketh my blood, dwelleth in me, and I in him. (John 6:55- 56)

The Purpose of the Covenant

The purpose of a covenant is to establish a relationship that is impossible to break. The covenant has procedures and customs which guarantee the relationship. It has both a curse to discourage breaking the relationship and a blessing to encourage loyalty. In God's covenant, His motivation for keeping His Word is His love, not the fear of a curse.

God is loyal and faithful, even when we are not. Human love without a covenant always has a self-preservation and self-protection quality about it. Human love is never totally unselfish apart from a covenant. It can never completely give of itself for fear of being hurt. But God's love gives and gives even when nothing is given in return.

Make the Blood Walk

Without a revelation of the blood covenant, you will never fully understand who you are in Christ or be able to accept the promises of the covenant for yourself. You will never understand this covenant book called the Bible.

The Hebrew word for God's love is *hesed*. The New Testament Greek equivalent is *agape*. Translators have had a hard time translating this word into English. It has been translated as "lovingkindness" and as "mercy," but these words are a far cry from its full meaning. *Hesed* means "unending loyalty with all of its implications." *Hesed* means that no matter what happens and no matter how little we give to Him in return, we will forever be at the forefront of God's thinking. Nothing will take precedence over His devotion toward us and His concern for our welfare.

Get alone in the presence of God, and make this blood walk with Him. Ask God to give you not only the revelation of the covenant, but also the revelation of the *hesed* that it is founded on. As you make the walk, imagine walking in the blood of Jesus up to your ankles. Walk the figure 8, representing infinity. Do not make a bunch of promises that you can't keep. Simply ask God to help you receive the promises the covenant represents.

Ask God to give you the strength to stand in the covenant, to hold up your end of the covenant. When you have finished the covenant ceremony with God, then take communion with Jesus, doing it in remembrance of the price Jesus paid for your redemption. Then understand that you are the righteousness of God Almighty through the blood of Jesus and you

46

are free from guilt. Then you can go boldly before the throne of God without spot or blemish, and no devil can touch you.

A covenant between two men is a desire for peace. A covenant between man and God is made not so we can be like spoiled children having anything we want, but so that all the provisions of the kingdom of God are available to us. The covenant is a means whereby God can provide and protect us. And in return, we love Him with all our hearts.

The Covenant Curse

The curse in the covenant is the enforcement clause of the contract. If you don't hold up your end of the covenant and you end up breaking it, the curse takes effect. The basic law of the curse is that you die. That's the only way you get out of a covenant. If you break the covenant, it's your family's responsibility to turn you over to the avenger. You can't break a covenant and live. The very ground you walk on is considered cursed.

God Cuts Covenant with Abraham

When God entered into the covenant with Abraham, several important events took place. God changed Abram and Sarai's names to Abraham and Sarah. When you cut covenant with God, you get a new name.

The Abrahamic covenant is the basis of Judaism and Christianity. It was sealed by circumcision. This covenant bound Abraham and his descendants by indissoluble ties to God, and it bound God to Abraham and his descendants by the same solemn token.

God Appears as *El Shaddai.* When Abraham was ninety-nine years old, God appeared to him as "God Almighty" or "*El Shaddai.*" He said to Abraham, "Walk before me and be thou perfect. And I will make my covenant between me and thee, and will multiply thee exceedingly" (Genesis 17:1–2).

We see Abraham on his face. God is talking with him and tells him, "As for me, behold, my covenant is with thee, and thou shalt be the father of a multitude of nations. Neither shall thy name any more be called Abram, but thy name shall be Abraham, for the father of a multitude of nations have I made thee" (Gen. 17:4–5).

A couple chapters earlier, God made a promise to Abraham, and it says that Abraham believed God "and He counted it to him for righteousness" (Gen. 15:6).

This word *believe* means that Abraham made an unqualified committal of himself and all he was or ever would be to God.

In the Hebrew it means not only a loving trust, but it also means "give yourself wholly up," or "to be a part of Himself," or "go right into Him," or "the unqualified committal."

Abraham gave himself totally to God, and God gave Himself totally to Abraham by cutting covenant with him.

Abraham Is Circumcised

In Genesis 17, God added to the covenant with Abraham through circumcision. This time Abraham was required to offer blood.

When that was done, God and Abraham entered into the covenant. This meant four things:

1. All Abraham had or ever would have was laid on the altar.
2. God must sustain and protect Abraham to the very limit of God's power.
3. When God cut the covenant with Abraham, the Israelite nation came into being as a covenant people as a result.
4. The covenant was limited to the seed of Abraham and had behind it the promise and the oath of God.

Covenant Facts

The seal of the covenant was circumcision. Every male child was circumcised when they were eight days old. This rite was the entrance into the covenant, causing that child to become an inheritor of everything connected with the covenant.

If the child's father and mother should die, another Israelite was under obligation to care for the child; or if the husband should die, to care for the widow.

It was said in ancient times in regard to the law of the covenant that all things were laid upon the altar. This meant that you were willing to give up or sacrifice whatever was necessary to honor the covenant. If keeping the covenant with a blood brother meant the death or loss of a wife or of a firstborn, the destruction of his property, or loss of his own life, everything was laid upon the altar.

Abraham's Sacrifice

God said to Abraham, "Take now thy son, thine only son Isaac, whom thou lovest" (Gen. 22:2).

There was no wavering on the part of Abraham. Consider what this meant to him. We know how he had longed for a son. We know how he had expressed his longings to God in those years when it seemed that such a possibility was gone forever. Then God promised him a son. Abraham was one hundred years old and Sarah was ninety. According to their knowledge, there was no way they could become parents of a natural child (see Gen. 18:11). But Abraham chose to not consider the facts, but to believe God. He believed God could make good on His promise. And He did: "And the Lord visited Sarah as he had said, and the Lord did unto Sarah as he had spoken. And Sarah conceived, and bare Abraham a son in his old age" (Gen. 21:1–2).

When Isaac was eighteen to twenty years old, God said to Abraham, "Take now thy son, thine only son, even Isaac, whom thou lovest unto a mountain which I will show thee and offer him there as a burnt offering" (Gen. 22:1–3). Abraham didn't hesitate, though it meant giving up all he held dear. He took Isaac on that three-day journey to Mt. Moriah, and together they built the altar. Abraham had laid Isaac on the altar and drew the knife to slay him when the angel of the Lord stopped him.

Because God knew that Abraham would keep the covenant, He said to Abraham, "By Myself have I sworn, for because thou hast not withheld thy son, thine only son; that in blessing I will bless thee, and in multiplying I will multiply thy seed as the stars of the heaven" (Gen. 22:16–17).

Note that God said, "By Myself have I sworn." God's throne became the surety of His promise.

Blessings of the Covenant

There were many blessings that came with God's covenant with Abraham and his lineage. Some of those blessings were:

1. God was under obligation to protect them from the armies of the nations that surrounded them.
2. God was under obligation to see that their land brought forth large crops.
3. God was under obligation by the covenant to see that their herds and flocks multiplied.
4. The hand of God was upon them in blessing.
5. They became the head of the nations, and with great wealth.
6. Jerusalem became the richest city the world had ever known. Their hillsides were irrigated and their valleys teemed with wealth. There was no city like it, no nation like it. God was their God, they were God's covenant people.
7. Under the covenant, one man could chase a thousand in war, and two could put ten thousand to flight. In David's day, when the covenant truth became a living force in the nation, David's blood-covenant warriors could individually slay eight hundred men in combat. They could rip a lion apart with their bare hands. They had divine protection that made them the greatest warriors the world ever knew.

8. They were God's peculiar people. They were the treasure of the heart of God.

We are the seed of Abraham; therefore, we have the right to partake of this awesome covenant. Every blessing belongs to us. And yet, as awesome as this covenant is, there is a new covenant that is founded on even better promises through the blood of Jesus Christ.

We see Jesus in the upper room on the night before His crucifixion. After He had blessed the bread and broken it, He said, "This is My body which is given for you" (Luke 22:19). Then He took a cup of wine and said, "This cup is the new testament [covenant] in my blood, which is shed for you" (Luke 22:20).

The old blood covenant was the basis on which the new covenant was founded. When Jesus said, "This is my blood of the new covenant," the disciples knew what it meant. They knew that when they cut the covenant with Jesus in that upper room that night, they had entered into the strongest, most sacred covenant known to the human heart.

The author of Hebrews said, "Then said he, Lo, I come to do thy will, O God. He taketh away the first, that he may establish the second" (Heb. 10:9).

As the old covenant was sealed with circumcision, the new covenant is sealed with the new birth. The old covenant had the Levitical priesthood. The new covenant has Jesus as the High Priest and we are the royal and holy priesthood (see 1 Peter 2:1–10).

The first priesthood had a temple in which God dwelt in the Holy of Holies with the ark of the covenant (see Exodus 40). In the new covenant, our bodies are the temple of God and the Spirit dwells within them.

God was the surety of the old covenant. But Hebrews 7:22 says, "By so much also hath Jesus become the surety of a better covenant."

Jesus stands behind every sentence in the new covenant. He is its great Intercessor: "He is able also to save them to the uttermost that come unto God by him, seeing he ever liveth to make intercession for them" (Heb. 7:25).

The Contrast of the Two Covenants

The Bible is composed of two covenants, contracts, or agreements. The first covenant was between Abraham and God. It was sealed by circumcision.

It is called the "Abrahamic covenant," and the Law that was given through Moses belonged to this covenant. When the Israelites were delivered from Egypt, they had no law nor government, so God gave them the Law. We call it the Mosaic Law. It is the covenant law, with its priesthood, sacrifices, ceremonies, and offerings.

The Law had no sooner been given than it was broken. Then God provided the atonement (covering) for the broken Law.

The word *atonement* means "to cover." It is not a New Testament word; it does not appear in the New Testament Greek. The blood of Jesus Christ cleanses instead of merely covering. The first covenant did not take away sin, it merely covered it. It didn't give eternal life or the new birth; it gave a promise of it. It didn't give fellowship with God; it gave a type of it.

It gave protection to Israel as a nation and it met their physical needs. God was Israel's Healer, Provider, and Protector.

You cannot separate Moses's Law from the covenant. So when the covenant was fulfilled, the Law was fulfilled and set aside. Sacrifices could never make man perfect under the covenant. The author of Hebrews says:

> For the law having a shadow of good things to come, and not the very image of the things, can never with those sacrifices which they offered year by year continually make the comers thereunto perfect. For then would they not have ceased to be offered? Because that the

worshippers once purged should have had no more conscience of sins. (Heb. 10:1–2)

The blood of bulls and goats did not cleanse the conscience, didn't take sin consciousness away from man. The inference is that there is a sacrifice that takes away the sin consciousness so that man stands un-condemned in God's presence. Paul tells us that that sacrifice is Jesus.

There is therefore now no condemnation to them that are in Christ Jesus. (Rom. 8:1)

Being therefore justified by faith, we have peace with God through our Lord Jesus Christ. (Rom. 5:1)

God becomes our Righteousness or our Justification, "that he might be just, and the justifier of him which believeth in Jesus" (Rom. 3:26).

The Abrahamic Covenant and the New Covenant

The Mosaic Law had the priesthood, the sacrifices, the ceremonies, and the offerings. The Abrahamic covenant gave provision, health, and protection. You cannot separate Moses's Law from the covenant, so when the covenant was fulfilled, the Law was fulfilled and set aside.

Additionally, Paul tells us, "Christ hath redeemed us from the curse of the law, being made a curse for us: for it is written, Cursed is every one that hangeth on a tree" (Gal. 3:13).

Christ took all of our sins upon Himself, on the cross, according to Colossians 2:14. He paid the price for our sins.

The next step that takes place is that God becomes our righteousness and he is the One who justifies us. This is such a crucial thing to understand as we study what Jesus did for us. Then Jesus takes it a step further and He becomes our advocate. Take a look at these verses about this.

To declare, I say, at this time his righteousness: that he might be just, and the justifier of him which believeth in Jesus. (Rom. 3:26)

Who shall lay anything to the charge of God's elect? It is God that justifieth. Who is he that condemneth? It is Christ that died, yea rather, that is risen again, who is even at the right hand of God, who also maketh intercession for us. (Rom. 8:33-34)

My little children, these things write I unto you, that ye sin not. And if any man sin, we have an advocate with the Father, Jesus Christ the righteous. (1 John 2:1)

Not Guilty

The author of Hebrews reminds us of God's promise: "And their sins and iniquities will I remember no more" (Heb. 10:17).

God's righteousness has been imparted to you not as an experience, but as a legal fact. God Almighty becomes your righteousness the moment you believe in the Lord Jesus Christ. That gives you a standing in the presence of the Father identical to the standing of Jesus. When you learn to walk as Jesus walked, without any consciousness of inferiority to God or satan, you will have faith that will stagger the world!

No, that does not make you equal with God—not by any stretch of the imagination. It does mean that you have every right to stand before God in all the rights, privileges, and benefits of a son.

Paul said to the Galatians, "I am crucified with Christ: nevertheless I live; yet not I, but Christ liveth in me: and the life which I now live in the flesh I live by the faith of the Son of God, who loved me, and gave himself for me" (Galatians 2:20).

I am in complete union with Christ Jesus (I am the branch, you are the vine), I depend entirely upon Him.

Come Boldly before the Throne of God

If it's true that all things are ours (see 1 Cor. 3:21), we are complete in Him (see Col. 2:9), and all things are beneath our feet (see Eph. 1:22), satan has been conquered, and we are more than conquerers through Him who loved us (see Rom. 8:37), then where is the place for begging and crying?

Brothers and Sisters, God created us in His image, He gave us the new covenant, redeeming us from the curse of the law, He gave us the name of Jesus (authority), He gave us miracle-working power through the baptism of the Holy Spirit, and He made us the righteousness of God Almighty. We are righteous, we are a holy priesthood. The devil has no grounds to accuse us. Take your rightful place in the kingdom of God. Come boldly before the throne of God and impact this world for Jesus Christ.

Purpose of Creation

Do not forget the original purpose of creation, which is to have an intimate relationship with God Almighty through His son Jesus Christ. It is all about the Father, the Son, and the Holy Spirit. Everything that God provided is so we can have that relationship with Him.

Take the time to read Deuteronomy chapters 26–30 and study and meditate what is being said, and recognize God's covenant with the nation of Israel. Ask the Holy Spirit to show you the heart of God in this covenant.

Another example of a biblical covenant was between David and Jonathan, King Saul's son (see 1 Samuel 18:3). Some twenty years later after Jonathan had died, David could not forget his obligation to the covenant they had made with each other. The covenant law demanded that the covenant was passed on to Jonathan's son. Only a true man of honor can enter into covenant. See what David did:

And David said, Is there yet any that is left of the house of Saul, that I may shew him kindness for Jonathan's sake? (2 Sam. 9:1)

David's servant Ziba told him about Jonathan's son Mephibosheth that lived in Lodebar. David sent for him immediately.

Now when Mephibosheth, the son of Jonathan, the son of Saul, was come unto David, he fell on his face, and did reverence. And David said, Mephibosheth. And he answered, Behold thy servant! And David said unto him, Fear not: for I will surely shew thee kindness for Jonathan thy father's sake, and will restore thee all the land of Saul thy father; and thou shalt eat bread at my table continually. (2 Sam. 9:6–7)

Covenant is no light thing. It is to be entered into with great respect. We must get that revelation with our covenant with Almighty God. Our covenant must be highly honored.

CHAPTER 4: THRESHOLD COVENANT

I n ancient times there were no temples or tabernacles. There wasn't a communal place where sacrifices would have been made. Because of this, houses were the place where sacrifices or covenants would have been made. It seems that the entryway to the home, or the house's threshold, would have been the place that was considered to be the altar for the home.

Sacrifices were commonly done when an honored guest was coming. In these cases the animal would be slaughtered at the entryway of the house and the blood poured across the threshold. When the guest arrived, they were asked to step over the blood line as they came into the home. This action, in itself, was an implied covenant with those who lived within the house. They were to step over it reverently, not stop on the blood line, which would show contemp for the person making the covenant.

If the guest entered the house in any other way than stepping over the bloodline on the threshold, there was no implied covenant made. Does this sound familiar? We see verses in Scripture that indicate this custom of covenant-making:

> Verily, verily, I say unto you, He that entereth not by the door into the sheepfold, but climbeth up some other way, the same is a thief and a robber. But he that entereth in by the door is the shepherd of the sheep. (John 10:1-2)

> I am the door: by me if any man enter in, he shall be saved, and shall go in and out, and find pasture. The thief

cometh not, but for to steal, and to kill, and to destroy: I
am come that they might have life, and that they might
have it more abundantly. (John 10:9-10)

Of how much sorer punishment, suppose ye, shall he
be thought worthy, who hath trodden underfoot the Son
of God, and hath counted the blood of the covenant,
wherewith he was sanctified, an unholy thing, and hath
done despite unto the Spirit of grace? (Heb. 10:29)

In Jerusalem when the father of the house took the lamb to the temple
to be sacrificed, he took the lamb to the door of the temple. This is where
the priest laid his hands on the lamb prior to the lamb being sacrificed.

In some cultures, you cannot not carry a dead body across the
threshold. If someone died inside a home or building, you had to cut
a hole in the wall and carry the body out that way. They also could not
carry the body over the threshold of the city gates. In the wall of the city
was a very small gate that the dead were carried out through, and people
are not allowed to enter the city through that small gate.

Even though you cannot carry a body across the threshold, in some
places it is an honor to be buried under the threshold. We see this in the
book of Revelation:

And when he had opened the fifth seal, I saw under the
altar the souls of them that were slain for the word of
God, and for the testimony which they held. (Rev. 6:9)

There is significance given to the foundation stone of a new building
being built. That stone is, in a sense, the threshold for the new structure.
Some ancient cultures would lay the foundational stones in blood, which
is a way of putting blood on the threshold. Earlier blood sacrifices for
this blood was sometimes done with humans, but later animals were
used for this foundation stone blood.

CHAPTER 4: THRESHOLD COVENANT

Sometimes the door of the house was not in the middle of a wall, but at the corner of the wall. In these instances, a large stone was placed in the corner that was used for cooking and fires. this was also the threshold so additionally it was the altar where animals were sacrificed in that home. Later on, this stone became known as the cornerstone, which was used to measure the whole foundation for the home. This is significant because if the cornerstone was not right, the rest of the measurements for the house would be off. The strength and integrity for the whole home depended on the cornerstone.

Paul tells us that Jesus is the chief cornerstone:

> Now therefore ye are no more strangers and foreigners, but fellow citizens with the saints, and of the household of God; "And are built upon the foundation of the apostles and prophets, Jesus Christ himself being the chief corner stone; In whom all the building fitly framed together groweth unto an holy temple in the Lord: In whom ye also are builded together for an habitation of God through the Spirit. (Eph. 2:19–22)

Peter also speaks of Jesus being the chief cornerstone:

> Wherefore also it is contained in the scripture, Behold, I lay in Sion a chief corner stone, elect, precious: and he that believeth on him shall not be confounded. Unto you therefore which believe he is precious: but unto them which be disobedient, the stone which the builders disallowed, the same is made the head of the corner, And a stone of stumbling, and a rock of offence, even to them which stumble at the word, being disobedient: whereunto also they were appointed. (1 Peter 2:6–8)

Peter is quoting from Isaiah here: "Therefore thus saith the Lord GOD, Behold, I lay in Zion for a foundation a stone, a tried stone, a precious corner stone, a sure foundation: he that believeth shall not make haste" (Isa. 28:16).

Try to imagine with me that you are inside the house and looking toward the door. Just to the left of the door is the cornerstone of the house. This is the rock (the altar) where the sacrifice is made. Paul said that we "are built upon the foundation of the apostles and prophets, Jesus Christ himself being the chief corner stone" (Eph. 2:20). Jesus also said that "upon this rock I will build my church" (Matt. 16:18).

On the rock lies the Lamb of God. "Behold the Lamb of God, which taketh away the sin of the world" (John 1:29). Just to the right of the altar you see the door with its threshold. Jesus said, "I am the door" (John 10:9). As you look at the Lamb of God lying on the rock, you can see His blood running down across the threshold and on the door. "For this is my blood of the new testament, which is shed for many for the remission of sins."

Then you see Jesus standing just outside the door. "Behold, I stand at the door, and knock: if any man hear my voice, and open the door, I will come in to him, and will sup with him, and he with me" (Revelation 3:20). Jesus is waiting for you to invite Him to step across that threshold covered with His blood thereby entering into covenant with you.

Once you have done that you complete the covenant with Him by eating the bread and drinking the wine (see Luke 22:19–20). Now you are in covenant with Jesus and you sit in Him at the right hand of God the Father in heavenly places (see Eph. 2:6).

Jesus provides the entire covenant. He is the Rock and the Lamb. It is His blood. He is the door and the threshold. Your only part is to invite Him to step over that threshold and accept Him into your heart and be born again, becoming one with Him forever.

So the question is, are we in the covenant, or are we trying to get into the covenant? Are we one with the Lord or are we trying to be one with Him?

We need to know what our position is in Christ and how we got there. Let's go back and break this down to see how we became one with Christ and how our old man was crucified with Christ.

The day that Adam broke the covenant with God, he died:

And the LORD God commanded the man, saying, Of every tree of the garden thou mayest freely eat: But of the tree of the knowledge of good and evil, thou shalt not eat of it: for in the day that thou eatest thereof thou shalt surely die. (Gen. 2:17)

Adam died that same day. First spiritually, then physically.

That is when God put His plan into effect. Not plan B—God only has plan A. He never gets caught off guard. God knows right where you are, and you are on schedule because God knew when you were going to be ready for the next step in His plan for your life. He is just waiting for you to get your head in the game so He can release awesome gifts and callings into your life to advance His kingdom.

God had a plan to save His creation, but it was going to take Him four days to pull it off. When God gave His instructions for the Passover He said on the tenth day of Abib that the spotless lamb is to be selected and separated, and then on the fourteenth day of Abib, the lamb is to be killed. Peter says that "one day is with the Lord as a thousand years, and a thousand years as one day" (2 Peter 3:8). So that is four days, or four thousand years, since Adam broke the covenant.

Only the Lamb of God could pay the price for our sins. Paul said, "Whom God hath set forth to be a propitiation through faith in his blood, to declare his righteousness for the remission of sins that are past, through the forbearance of God" (Rom. 3:25). Paul is saying here that God sent His son Jesus to be the propitiation through faith in His blood to declare His righteousness for the remission of our sins.

Propitiation: An Atoning Sacrifice

An atoning sacrifice is preformed to cause an offended person to become disposed to be gracious or merciful, ready to forgive sins and bestow blessings. Jesus was the ultimate propitiation:

And he is the propitiation for our sins: and not for ours only, but also for the sins of the whole world. (1 John 2:2)

Herein is love, not that we loved God, but that he loved us, and sent his Son to be the propitiation for our sins. (1 John 4:10)

In Romans chapter 3, the apostle Paul shows us that Christ's death is a propitiatory sacrifice that acted as God's righteous vindication of "passing over" sins, which was the only way that sin could be passed over righteously.

Being justified freely by his grace through the redemption that is in Christ Jesus: whom God set forth to be a propitiation, through faith, by his blood, to show his righteousness, because of the passing over of the past sins, in the forbearance of God. (Rom. 3:20).

Then in Hebrews chapter 9 we see that Christ's propitiation can only come by faith, and that any person who accept Christ's sacrifice as payment for their sins become possessed by the "righteousness of God" and are perfectly justified in the sight of God.

For if the blood of bulls and of goats, and the ashes of an heifer sprinkling the unclean, sanctifieth to the purifying of the flesh: How much more shall the blood of Christ, who through the eternal Spirit offered himself without spot to God, purge your conscience from dead works to serve the living God? (Heb. 9:13-14)

So through the death of Christ, there is power to be free of guilt, for sinners to be redeemed from condemnation and to be put back into right relation with God, therefore granting God's favor over their life.

So how did this happen? The following five scriptures put together gives an outline for how it was done:

I am crucified with Christ: nevertheless I live; yet not I, but Christ liveth in me: and the life which I now live in the flesh

I live by the faith of the Son of God, who loved me, and gave himself for me. (Gal. 2:20)

Blotting out the handwriting of ordinances that was against us, which was contrary to us, and took it out of the way, nailing it to his cross. (Col. 2:14)

Christ hath redeemed us from the curse of the law, being made a curse for us: for it is written, Cursed is every one that hangeth on a tree. (Gal. 3:13)

Buried with him in baptism, wherein also ye are risen with him through the faith of the operation of God, who hath raised him from the dead. (Col. 2:12)

Therefore if any man be in Christ, he is a new creature: old things are passed away; behold, all things are become new. (2 Cor. 5:17)

In essence, what the verses above are saying is when I asked Jesus to come into my heart, He took hold of me and Almighty God at the same time, and the very essence of God began to pour into me. My old man was crucified, my dead spirit came alive and I was born again, and I became a new creation in Christ. The essence of God was so overwhelming that I was crucified with Christ and my old man was gone forever. Now my life is dependent not on my faith, but by the faith of the Son of God, who loved me and gave himself for me. Therefore being in Christ, I am a new creature, a creation that never existed before, the old man has passed away and all things have become new.

The Bible says that Jesus was the mediator of a better covenant. He was the perfect sacrifice. The law of the covenant has been satisfied. The old man that broke the covenant has been killed, complying with the law of covenant, and has been buried. You were born again and raised with Christ, a new man in Christ Jesus.

Not only am I one with Almighty God, but His glory is in me: "And the glory which thou gavest me I have given them; that they may be one, even as we are one" (John 17:22). And because He lives in me, there is a power to be a witness to the world that I did not possess before.

> But ye shall receive power, after that the Holy Ghost is come upon you: and ye shall be witnesses unto me both in Jerusalem, and in all Judaea, and in Samaria, and unto the uttermost part of the earth. (Acts 1:8)

This is what sets us apart from all other religions. We serve a living God. A God that lives in us and we are one with Him. He demonstrates his love for His creation by doing miracles through His saints.

What the heathen attempted to do with their bloodletting and blood sacrifices, trying to be one with their god, we have accomplished through the blood of Jesus Christ. We are no longer trying to become one with our God, because we have attained to the very righteousness of God Almighty through faith in the blood of Jesus Christ. We stand before Him in the spotless Lamb of God carrying His name where ever we go.

Jesus said "*tetelestai*" on the cross just before giving up the ghost, which means "paid in full."

Accept it, receive it; it is done! You are in full covenant with Almighty God, fully deserving of all rights, privileges, and benefits of the kingdom of God.

Now walk in it!

CHAPTER 5: SALT COVENANT

We have established that God first made a blood covenant with Adam in the garden of Eden, then with Noah after the flood, and then with Abraham, Isaac, and Jacob. It was reestablished with Moses and the giving of the Law, then with David and his son Solomon, and many other kings, right up to Jesus dying on the cross.

But when God made a covenant with King David, He did it differently than with the others. This covenant was an everlasting one: the covenant of salt (see 2 Sam. 23:5; 2 Chron. 13:5).

An ancient Jewish commentary adds: "For as the waters of the sea never grow sweet, neither shall the dominion depart from the house of David."[16]

Adam Clarke's Commentary on the Bible offers the following on this covenant:

> It is a covenant of salt—That is, an incorruptible, everlasting covenant. As salt was added to different kinds of foods not only to give them flavor but to preserve them from decay it became the emblem of incorruptibility and permanence. Hence, a covenant of salt signified an everlasting covenant. Among the Asiatics, eating together was deemed a bond of perpetual friendship; and as salt was

---

16. Clarke, Adam, "Commentary on 2 Chronicles 13:5," *The Adam Clarke Commentary,* (T. Mason and G Lane: New York, 1837).

a common article in all their meals it may be in reference to this circumstance that a perpetual covenant is termed a covenant of salt; because the parties ate together of the sacrifice offered on the occasion and the whole transaction was considered as a league of endless friendship.[17]

The Lord told the priests that with all their offerings they were to offer salt. Salt was the opposite of leaven, for it preserved from decay and corruption and signified the purity and persevering faithfulness that was necessary for the worship of God. Everything was seasoned with it to signify the purity and perfection that should be extended through every part of the divine service and the hearts and lives of God's worshippers.

It was called the salt covenant of God, because as salt is incorruptible; so was the covenant made with Abram, Isaac, Jacob, and the patriarchs relative to the redemption of the world by the incarnation and death of Jesus Christ.

Among the heathens, salt was a common ingredient in all their sacrificial offerings; and as it was considered essential to the comfort and preservation of life, so it was supposed to be one of the most acceptable presents they could make unto their gods, from whose sacrifices it was never absent. [18]

God instructed Aaron that with every meat offering he was to include salt (see Lev. 2:13). The salt and the wood for the sacrifices were the responsibility of the congregation.

What is required of the 21ˢᵗ Century Church today?

Ye are the salt of the earth: but if the salt have lost his savor, wherewith shall it be salted? it is thenceforth good for nothing, but to be cast out, and to be trodden under foot of men. (Matt. 5:13)

17. Clarke, Adam, "Commentary on Numbers 18:19," *The Adam Clarke Commentary*, (T. Mason and G Lane: New York, 1837).

18. Clarke, Adam, "Commentary on Leviticus 2:13," *The Adam Clarke Commentary*, (T. Mason and G Lane:New York, 1837).

CHAPTER 5: SALT COVENANT

Just as salt influences whatever it touches, as born-again children of God, we should be influencing our surroundings. Salt preserves and prevents corruption, and our influence should do the same thing, beginning in our own families and then reaching out to the world.

In those days, when salt lost its savor, it was sometimes used on the roads. It would draw moisture, compact the ground, and make a kind of pavement.

If we are indeed salty, we will prevent corruption. Paul speaks of this in his letters to the Ephesians and the Colossians:

> Let no corrupt communication proceed out of your mouth, but that which is good to the use of edifying, that it may minister grace unto the hearers. And grieve not the holy Spirit of God, whereby ye are sealed unto the day of redemption. Let all bitterness, and wrath, and anger, and clamour, and evil speaking, be put away from you, with all malice: And be ye kind one to another, tenderhearted, forgiving one another, even as God for Christ's sake hath forgiven you. (Eph. 4:29–32)

> Let your speech be always with grace, seasoned with salt, that ye may know how ye ought to answer every man. (Col. 4:32)

Salt represents blood and life and could be substituted for blood on the threshold. When two people shared salt, it was considered a covenant. Enemies who shared salt could no longer be enemies. If you shared a meal with someone where salt was in the food or bread, it was considered a covenant. The covenant was considered to also be valid as long as the salt was in the body, which normally took up to twenty-four hours for the salt to pass through the body.

Have you ever asked why Lot's wife was transformed into a pillar of salt? Scholars trace this phenomenon back to the divine messengers who came to warn Lot of Sodom's upcoming doom. After their arrival,

Lot's wife ventures to a neighbor's house presuming to ask for salt, but using this as a means of betraying the visitors to the city. Because she sinned through salt, her judgment came through salt.

Among those who know about salt being a substitute for blood, you will find that sometimes they will use salt instead of the unity candle at weddings. The bride and the groom will each have their container of salt and will pour together into a larger single container, thereby mixing the two becoming one. It is said then that the covenant can no more be broken than you can separate the grains of salt and put them back into their original container. I like this better than the unity candle because it is a much stronger visual of the covenant.

As we have seen, there are several ways you can make a blood covenant:

1. By cutting the flesh and the two making covenant putting the cut flesh together thereby receiving each other's blood into their bodies becoming one with each other.
2. By using a substitute to do the covenant the same way.
3. By sharing a covenant meal.
4. By pouring blood over the threshold and stepping over the blood entering into the covenant.
5. By pouring salt over the threshold and stepping over the threshold entering into the covenant.
6. By sharing salt with someone you enter into covenant.

Whatever way that you do it, it is held to be very sacred and must not be entered into lightly. This is why you never enter into covenant with anyone who does not have the highest of integrity. God chose to enter into a covenant with you. You are His bride and He is depending on you to hold up your end of the covenant with the highest respect.

CHAPTER 6: *HESED*

I realize that most people that are reading this book have never heard this word *hesed* before. It is a beautiful and rich word in the Hebrew language that powerfully describes the faithful mercy and steadfast lovingkindness of our Lord. It speaks of a level of love that Almighty God has for His creation that is so wonderful that the English language cannot describe the height, the depth, or the weight of it. It is the kind of love that compelled God to send His only Son to the earth to suffer terribly and to be crucified, paying the penalty for our crime of breaking the covenant, making a way to be redeemed making us the righteousness of God Almighty. And because this *hesed* is so great and powerful, we now sit at the right hand of Almighty God in Christ Jesus, saved, sanctified, and bathed in His precious blood, wearing pure white robes furnished by Him.

Hesed is the unconditional, God-level of love that He has for His creation. It is mentioned over 245 times in the Old Testament, and it is always connected to the covenant. You can have *hesed* for someone without being in covenant with them, but you cannot be in covenant with someone and not have *hesed* for them.

Covenant, *hesed*, and truth are always bonded together. When you have Hesed for someone you always look out for their best interest. You always put them first. You are willing to sacrifice everything, including your own life, for them. They are always at the forefront of your thoughts.

Hesed and Truth

Truth is paramount in this relationship. You would never think of misleading, much less lying to the person that you are in covenant with or have *hesed* for. This is why you should never enter into a covenant with someone who is lacking in character or integrity. The person who is selfish or self-centered will always break the covenant. The Bible warns us to be careful who we covenant with:

> Be ye not unequally yoked together with unbelievers: for what fellowship hath righteousness with unrighteousness? and what communion hath light with darkness? (2 Cor. 6:14)

> Thou shalt not plow with an ox and an ass together. (Deut. 22:10)

> Can two walk together, except they be agreed? (Amos 3:3)

If you are going to be in covenant with someone, you must be of one mind.

> And what concord hath Christ with Belial? or what part hath he that believeth with an infidel? And what agreement hath the temple of God with idols? for ye are the temple of the living God; as God hath said, I will dwell in them, and walk in them; and I will be their God, and they shall be my people. Wherefore come out from among them, and be ye separate, saith the Lord, and touch not the unclean thing; and I will receive you [take into favor]. And will be a Father unto you, and ye shall be my sons and daughters, saith the Lord Almighty. (2 Cor. 6:15–18)

Always On His Mind

You are in covenant with Almighty God, therefore He always has you at the forefront of His thoughts: "For I know the thoughts that I think toward you, saith the LORD, thoughts of peace, and not of evil, to give you an expected end" (Jer. 29:11).

This is how I translate this scripture from the original Hebrew: "For I know the plan that I purpose toward you, saith the Lord. Plans of

Shalom, and not of evil, to cause you without fail the thing that I long for in your posterity or future."

You are always at the forefront of His mind. He is always looking for a way to bless you. He is always looking out for you and your best interest.

Many times in the Psalms *hesed* is translated as "mercy." Here are just a few of them:

> All the paths of the LORD are mercy [*hesed*] and truth unto such as keep his covenant and his testimonies. (Ps. 25:10)

> Many sorrows shall be to the wicked: but he that trusteth in the LORD, mercy [*hesed*] shall compass him about. (Ps. 32:10)

> When I said, My foot slippeth; thy mercy [*hesed*], O LORD, held me up. (Ps. 94:18)

> Surely goodness and mercy [*hesed*] shall follow me all the days of my life: and I will dwell in the house of the LORD forever. (Ps. 23:6)

Returning *Hesed* to God

God is going out of His way to bring *hesed* and truth into your life, but *hesed*, like covenant, works both ways. As He deals with you with *hesed* and truth, you are expected to deal with Him with *hesed* and truth as well. We must learn to return *hesed* to Him.

God says that the church is the bride of Christ. How would our marriage be if we took our spouse for granted, never spent any time with them, and never talked to them about our life or showed interest in theirs?

For many Christians, the only time they spend with the Holy Spirit is when they go to church. Many are not taught so they don't know how to show affection for the Holy Spirit, for God, or for Jesus. They don't know how to have a relationship with Him. To be taught is one reason we go to church, but church is more than a bunch of people gathering together to hear someone preach.

The first thing we do is worship God. It's much more than just a singalong. This should be the primary reason we go to church. It's during praise and worship that we give God our love through our worship. If you don't do anything else at church, you should be doing this.

It's amazing to me that the modern-day Christian believes that preaching is the important part of having church. It's not—it's the least important part.

Giving glory and honor to God is the most important thing we can do. The last thing I want to do is try to teach behind a worship service where the Holy Spirit was taken for granted and therefore didn't manifest Himself. We should worship until the glory of God comes—and never limit the Holy Spirit.

One of the things we can do to show Him honor is to be on time. I knew a woman one time who told me that she just couldn't make it on time on Sunday morning. She said she had four kids and a husband to get dressed and get them to church. But I noticed that on Black Friday, she was in front of the electronics store at four in the morning. One thing I have learned in life is that you may not have time to do everything you want to do, but you will always have time to do what is important to you.

So that begs the question, what is the priority in your life? Or let me put it another way—*who* is the priority in your life? I need to ask myself: do I have a specific time every day that I give God? I don't mean prayer at bedtime. Do I have an appointment every day with God so that just He and I can talk? A time where I can tell Him how much I love and appreciate Him and thank Him for all He has done for me? This is not when I give Him my list of needs in my life. This is when I just want to be with Him, enjoying His presence. I just want to love Him and worship Him. After I do that, when I go to church I can easily step over into worship because I have been worshipping Him all week.

I'm trying to teach you what God desires from you. He wants your love. *Hesed* works both ways. We need to try to show Him as much *hesed* as He shows us. This is how covenant works; this is how *hesed* works; this is how truth works. We give back as much as we get.

We are always at the forefront of His mind. He desires to be a Father to us and He wants us to be His sons and daughters. Surely His goodness and *hesed* are in hot pursuit with immediate intent all the days of our life. We must learn how to give God *hesed*.

This is *hesed* to God:

> Thou shalt love the Lord thy God with all thy heart, and with all thy soul, and with all thy mind. This is the first and great commandment. And the second is like unto it, Thou shalt love thy neighbour as thyself. On these two commandments hang all the law and the prophets. (Matt. 22:37–40)

> He hath shewed thee, O man, what is good; and what doth the LORD require of thee, but to do justly, and to love mercy [*hesed*], and to walk humbly with thy God? (Micah 6:8)

> For I desired mercy [*hesed*], and not sacrifice; and the knowledge of God more than burnt offerings. (Hos. 6:6)

Additionally, Paul said in Philippians 2:3 that we are to esteem others greater than ourselves.

Hesed always considers the other person's needs as greater than their own; they always come first.

Hesed and Covenant

It is not enough that we are aware or have knowledge of these covenant principles. We must internalize them until they come alive in us and we walk in the revelation of the truth of God's word. *Hesed* is so connected to the covenant that it must be embraced and honored and most of all practiced in our daily life. Covenant, *hesed*, and truth are one. They cannot be separated any more than you can separate God the Father, God the Son, and God the Holy Spirit. If you remove any one of them, you don't have any of them.

We need this principle working in our lives now more than we ever have. We are living in the perilous times that Paul warned us about. We are most definitely in the last days. Paul describes what is going on around us today in 2 Timothy 3. As kingdom citizens, we have a responsibility to develop these principles in our life.

Covenant *hesed* is a two-sided coin. We've looked at the blessing side of the covenant, now we must consider the curse side. The obvious question to be asked is, "Will God continue to demonstrate His covenant loyalty and *hesed* when a person lives in continuous and blatant sin without repentance?" We find that answer in the book of Jeremiah. The Lord removed His *hesed* from Judah during the days of Jeremiah because they were not faithful to the covenant:

> I have taken away My peace from this people, saith the LORD, even lovingkindness [hesed] and mercies. (Jer. 16:5)

> Wherefore hath the Lord pronounced all this great evil against us? . . . Because your fathers have forsaken me, saith the LORD, and have walked after other gods, and have served them, and have worshipped them, and have forsaken me, and have not kept my law; And ye have done worse than your fathers; for, behold, ye walk every one after the imagination of his evil heart, that they may not hearken unto me. (Jer. 16:10–12)

74

Again in the book of Hosea, God rejects Israel because Israel has turned her back on God.

> Hear the word of the LORD, ye children of Israel: for the LORD hath a controversy with the inhabitants of the land, because there is no truth, nor mercy [*hesed*], nor knowledge of God in the land. (Hosea 4:1)

> My people are destroyed for lack of knowledge: because thou hast rejected knowledge, I will also reject thee, that thou shalt be no priest to me: seeing thou hast forgotten the law of thy God, I will also forget thy children. (Hosea 4:6)

God is saying that if we do not faithfully observe *hesed* and walk in honor of the covenant, He will not only reject us, but He will also reject our children. If we are unfaithful to the covenant, then we are subject to punishment and God's *hesed* will be removed, but if we are faithful God will be faithful to us.

The prophet Nehemiah said, "I beseech thee, O LORD God of heaven, the great and terrible God, that keepeth covenant and mercy [*hesed*] for them that love him and observe his commandments" (Nehemiah 1:5). To keep and observe His commandments is to not only to know them, but to walk in them consciously. We do this on purpose with intent. We are determined to please our God and show Him honor. Just as David was compelled to honor his covenant with Jonathan by blessing his son Mephibosheth, we must honor the covenant we have with Almighty God through our substitute Jesus Christ. We must not dishonor the blood of Jesus Christ.

> Of how much sorer punishment, suppose ye, shall he be thought worthy, who hath trodden underfoot the Son of God, and hath counted the blood of the covenant, wherewith he was sanctified, an unholy thing, and hath done despite unto the Spirit of grace? (Heb. 10:29)

A Prophetic Word

As I was writing this, the Holy Spirit spoke this prophetic word through my wife, Susan:

> "You are more than a number in a gathering of people. You are a kingdom-of-God citizen, you have a kingdom purpose and assignment. The kingdom of God has need of you. You are in this kingdom for such a time as this. Move with the Holy Spirit. Hear, heed, and obey. As you do, your life will be enriched and fruitful in seeing others transformed and made whole. This will keep you in the center of the will of God, causing Jesus to be famous on the earth. Let Him be glorified in all you do."

This is so amazing. Even now as I am writing God is showing His *hesed* to you and me. To everyone reading this, that prophetic word is spoken directly to you. Can you not see how important you are to God? You are always at the forefront of God's mind!

CHAPTER 7: SALVATION MANIFESTED IN ITS HIGHEST FORM

T he word *salvation* is translated from the Greek word *soteria*. It means "deliverance, preservation, safety."[19] The word *saved* is translated from the Greek word *sozo* and its meaning is similar to salvation: "to save, to keep safe and sound, to rescue from danger or destruction."[20] Notice that both definitions speak of being delivered from or out of something, or being rescued from or out of something.

Let's look at a couple verses about salvation, replacing *salvation* with *deliverance* and *saved* with *rescue*. First we will look at Acts 4:12:

> Neither is there [deliverance] in any other: for there is none other name under heaven given among men, whereby we must be [rescued].

Let us also look at Romans 10:13 and do the same thing:

> For whosoever shall call upon the name of the Lord shall be [rescued].

As we read these scriptures we can see that the author is saying that we have been delivered, rescued, and saved from something, but what is it that we have been rescued from?

19. Brown-Driver-Briggs' Hebrew Definitions, s.v. *soteria,* 1906, public domain.

20. Brown-Driver-Briggs' Hebrew Definitions, s.v. *sozo,* 1906, public domain.

First I want to tell you that *soteria* or *sozo* is not your ticket to ride the Glory Train to heaven when you die. That ticket was punched the moment you were born again. Salvation is the benefit that came out of the born-again experience. It has nothing to do with going to heaven. There is nothing in heaven that you need to be delivered from. It is the evil of this world that we need deliverance from. One of the benefits of being born again is salvation. Jesus made that available to us.

As you now know from our previous study, there are both blessings and curses associated with covenant. If you obey the covenant and do not break it, you will receive blessings, but if you break the covenant, you will receive the curses. Before we were born again we had broken the covenant and were living under the curse. That is the law of the covenant—if you break it, you have to die.

> Behold, I set before you this day a blessing and a curse; A blessing, if ye obey the commandments of the LORD your God, which I command you this day: And a curse, if ye will not obey the commandments of the LORD your God, but turn aside out of the way which I command you this day, to go after other gods, which ye have not known. (Deut. 11:26–28)

> I call heaven and earth to record this day against you, that I have set before you life and death, blessing and cursing: therefore choose life, that both thou and thy seed may live. (Deut. 30:19)

The curse is the penalty for breaking the Law. The curse of the Law brings poverty, sickness, and death (see Deuteronomy 27:15–26; 28:15–68).

But there is good news—we have chosen Him, and therefore, we are rescued from the curse of the law. Jesus paid that price for us and redeemed us. The law of the covenant was satisfied; therefore we, being born again, were translated into the kingdom of God, and all the blessings of the covenant are available to us.

> Christ hath redeemed us from the curse of the law, being
> made a curse for us: for it is written, Cursed is every one that
> hangeth on a tree: That the blessing of Abraham might come
> on the Gentiles through Jesus Christ; that we might receive
> the promise of the Spirit through faith. (Gal. 3:13-14)

Verse 13 could be translated, "Christ hath exceedingly, abundantly above, vehemently done what was necessary to pay the price for our ransom from the curse of the law."

When we were born again, Peter said that we were called out of darkness into His marvelous light (see 1 Peter 2:9). When that happened, we entered into a covenant with Jesus, and that is what salvation comes out of. You will find that anytime we are blessed by God it will always be tied to covenant.

> For this is my blood of the New Testament, which is shed
> for many for the remission of sins. (Matt. 26:28)

The writer of Hebrews speaks of a better covenant with better promises.

> But now hath he obtained a more excellent ministry, by
> how much also he is the mediator of a better covenant,
> which was established upon better promises. (Heb. 8:6)

What are these better promises? He took away all of our sins, all of our failures, and all of our shame.

> Blotting out the handwriting of ordinances that was
> against us, which was contrary to us, and took it out of
> the way, nailing it to his cross. (Col. 2:14)

The Benefits of Simple Obedience

What does God expect of us in observing His covenant? What are His requirements for honoring His covenant, and thereby honoring Him?

And now, Israel, what doth the LORD thy God require of thee, but to fear the LORD thy God, to walk in all his ways, and to love him, and to serve the LORD thy God with all thy heart and with all thy soul, To keep the commandments of the LORD, and his statutes, which I command thee this day for thy good? (Deut. 10:12–13)

What God asked of us is not complicated; it's not beyond our ability to accomplish, and it's not hidden in vague words or phrases. It is simply obedience.

For I desired mercy [*hesed*], and not sacrifice; and the knowledge of God more than burnt offerings. (Hosea 6:6)

The Lord desires your undying love and He wants you to know Him—close intimate knowledge of Him. He wants you to come and sit on that special couch with Him. He even took the time to show you how to choose what is best for you.

One day as I was studying and meditating the Word of God, the Lord began to speak to me about salvation. He said: "Salvation manifested in its highest form is abundant provision, divine health, and the Zoe life of God Almighty manifested in you in His full and complete power and glory."

Now that we have been delivered out of darkness into His marvelous light, these are the awesome benefits that are available to us while we are still in this world. We need salvation here on the earth, we won't need it in heaven. There is no evil there.

I will take each one of these benefits—*abundant provision, divine health, and the Zoe life of God Almighty*—and show them to you in scripture. Remember I taught you that scripture is interpreted with scripture, and whatever you get prophetically has to line up with the Word of God. We will begin with abundant provision.

Abundant Provision

Abundant provision comes directly from the covenant. The provisions are laid out in Deuteronomy 28:1–14. I encourage you to read each one of them. If you don't know what it says is yours, how can you expect to receive the benefits? How do you make a claim for something that you don't know anything about?

Remember, "Everything God does is according to a pattern and based on a principle." The principle is the covenant and the pattern is found in Matt. 6:33: "But seek ye first the kingdom of God, and his righteousness; and all these things shall be added unto you."

You have to work the pattern; you must go after the kingdom of God. All of the benefits of salvation are found in the kingdom, so when you get into the kingdom you cross over into the benefits. You have been made the righteousness of God Almighty, so you have the right to make a demand on your benefits.

Divine Health

As abundant provision comes directly from the covenant, so also does divine health.

> And the LORD will take away from thee all sickness, and will put none of the evil diseases of Egypt, which thou knowest, upon thee; but will lay them upon all them that hate thee. (Deut. 7:15)

This should answer the question of, "does God put sickness on people to teach them a lesson?" I don't know how many times I have heard this, and as you can see, God said He would not put sickness on His people. He did, however, give us a clue as to why we have sickness on us.

In the book of John, Jesus heals a lame man by a pool called Bethesda. After He healed him, "Jesus findeth him in the temple, and said unto him, Behold, thou art made whole: sin no more, lest a worse thing come unto thee" (John 5:14).

Sin in our lives opens the door to sickness and disease. As long as there is sin in this world, there will be sickness and disease. However, just because a person is sick doesn't mean that that person is living in sin. God said that He would not put sickness on us and His Word is truth, so we cannot blame God when we get sick. The problem is that there is much sin in the world, so it is going to be very hard for most people to avoid all sickness.

Elisha was a great prophet of God and he still died from a sickness. Many variables bring about sickness. One example that is easy to show is that people who carry bitterness and unforgiveness opens the door to rheumatoid arthritis. I believe you will find that doctors will confirm this.

Peter says that being delivered from sickness and disease is part of our benefits of salvation: "Who his own self bare our sins in his own body on the tree, that we, being dead to sins, should live unto righteousness: by whose stripes ye were healed" (1 Peter 2:24). Our challenge is having the faith to believe God for our healing.

God has healed me many times. When I have had colds or the flu, the Lord has healed me during praise and worship in church. I would be caught up in worship and wouldn't notice that God had healed me, but would realize it afterward. He has given me two notable miracles in my body. Once when my foot had to be operated on, and another time when my back went out on me.

I had a plantar wart in the bottom of my foot which caused me a lot of discomfort. It was like walking with a piece of sharp gravel in my shoe. I put up with that for months, all the while believing God for a miracle to heal my foot. The miracle never came, so out of desperation I gave up on faith and went to the doctor. This was over twenty years ago while I was still working a full-time job. The doctor put me on the table and proceeded to cut open my foot and take out the plantar wart.

What I didn't realize was that I wouldn't be able to walk for five days after the procedure. The doctor didn't tell me that until he had cut me open. Now I was in a panic because I couldn't afford to miss work. I was at a total loss as to what I was going to do. The doctor gave me pain pills and told me that I should take one right then and that night set them by my bed because I would wake up during the night in pain.

I didn't wake up all night. The next morning when I awoke, I noticed that there was no pain in my foot. I sat on the side of my bed and pulled my foot up to be able to feel the bottom, and when I rubbed it, I felt no pain. Then I pulled off the bandage and felt of the bottom of my foot again. I couldn't feel anything, and when I pressed on the spot that had been cut, there was no pain. That's when I turned on the light. What I saw was so amazing that I just began to praise God. There was not a single mark on my foot! The stitches that the doctor had sewn were not there. There was not even a hint of a scar where he had cut me open! You couldn't tell that my foot had been touched.

I know what you're thinking. "Why didn't God heal him before he went to the doctor?" I don't have the answer to that question, but several years later God gave me another notable miracle very much the same way.

My back went out on me and I was in so much pain that I could just barely do my job. Like the last time, I was believing God for a miracle. Just as before, when I couldn't stand it any longer I went to the doctor. They gave me an MRI and found that I had three ruptured disks and a herniated disk. The doctor gave me a shot in my back and pain pills, but neither stopped the pain. I told God that I had to work, so I would just press through the pain and go to work. The pain was terrible, but I was determined to trust God and believe that He would do something to help me.

I had been off work for two weeks and in order to go back to work, I had to convince the company doctor that I could do my job. I did a great job of acting, and the doctor released me to go back to work so the next day I did.

My plan was to first just get to my workstation, and then I would figure out how to do my job. My mind was made up; I wasn't going to quit. The pain was terrible, but I pushed through it and began to work. That's when He did it. I heard the Holy Spirit say to me in that quiet, still voice of His, "Worship Him." I immediately put up my hands and began to worship Him, and was instantly healed!

I learned two lessons from these two miracles. One, never give up on God, and two, we must have a close intimate relationship with the Lord. Had I not heard His voice and obeyed Him instantly, I believe I would still be in pain.

What was also amazing is that in both cases, from time to time I was laying hands on people and seeing miracle healing for them. Healing is available to all of us, but it doesn't necessarily come easily. We have to develop our faith for healing. So how do we develop our faith?

The Apostle Paul said that " faith cometh by hearing, and hearing by the word of God" (Rom. 10:17). It is not just any word of God; it is the *rhema* word of God—the revelation of God. You study and meditate on the Word until it becomes a revelation to you and then you will have the faith necessary to receive your healing. Simply reading the Word of God without receiving revelation does not build faith.

Divine health is available to the born-again Christian. It is not easily achieved, but yet it is one of our benefits through salvation.

The *Zoe* Life of God Almighty

The *zoe* life of God Almighty manifested in you in His full and complete power and glory.

Jesus said to us, "I am come that they might have life and have it more abundantly" (John 10:10). That word *life* is translated from the Greek word *zoe*.

Can you imagine that? Jesus says that we can have life as God has life. That is hard to get your head around. He also said that we would own and possess this life as God has it. The phrase "might have" in this verse is translated from the Greek word *echo*, which means "to own or to possess."[21] Jesus doesn't stop there, He goes on to say that not only can we have life as God has it, but we can have it more abundantly. The word *abundantly* is translated from the Greek word *perisseuo*, which means "superabundant in quantity, superior in quality, beyond measure, superfluous."[22]

When the Lord was showing me this revelation, I began to wonder "How can a man walk in these realms with God? Is it possible?" As I was pondering these things, He reminded me of what He had already shown me in the scripture. In Psalm 8:5 He said that He created us just a little lower than Himself, *Elohiym*, the God who calls things that are not as though they were, the creator God.

We were created to be like Him. He created us in His image and after His likeness (see Gen. 1:26–27). We were meant to be like Him. We may not be walking in the fullness of the *zoe* life of God Almighty, but we can do better than we are doing. I believe that God wants us to seek after it with all our hearts.

You can have the *zoe* life of God Almighty manifested in you, in His full and complete power and glory. The word *full* means it's all there, there is no more room for anything else, and the word *complete* means that nothing is lacking. The entire life of God Almighty is available to you, there is nothing left out or kept from you. He holds nothing back.

> For the LORD God is a sun and shield: the LORD will give grace and glory: no good thing will he withhold from them that walk uprightly. (Ps. 84:11)

Power

All of this is manifested in you in His full and complete power. We find three kinds of power spoken of in the word of God. There is:

---

21. Thayer and Smith, "Greek Lexicon entry for Echo," The KJV New Testament Greek Lexicon, accessed November 11, 2020, https://www.biblestudytools.com/lexicons/greek/kjv/echo.html.

22. Strong's Hebrew and Greek Dictionaries, s.v. "*perisseuo*," 1890, public domain.

- *dunamis*, or miracle-working power;
- *exousia*, or authority; and
- *kratos*, or dominion.

Dunamis: Miraculous Power

> And, behold, I send the promise of my Father upon you:
> but tarry ye in the city of Jerusalem, until ye be endued
> with power [*dunamis*] from on high. (Luke 24:49)

Jesus is telling His disciples to wait in Jerusalem until they have received this miracle-working power. This power was coming to them through the baptism of the Holy Spirit, which was the promise of the Father.

> But ye shall receive power, after that the Holy Ghost is
> come upon you: and ye shall be witnesses unto me both
> in Jerusalem, and in all Judea, and in Samaria, and unto
> the uttermost part of the earth. (Acts 1:8)

All born again sons and daughters of God should receive the baptism of the Holy Spirit because that is where the *dunamis*, miracle-working power comes from, that is when you get it. Jesus did no miracles until He was baptized in the Holy Spirit. Let's look at the story of His baptism in Matthew 3:16:

> And Jesus, when he was baptized, went up straightway
> out of the water: and, lo, the heavens were opened unto
> him, and he saw the Spirit of God descending like a dove,
> and lighting upon him.

Jesus's example shows us that we are to be water baptized and baptized in the Spirit. After He was baptized in water by John, he went into the wilderness for forty days and nights to be tested. The Word says that when He returned, He "returned in the power [*dunamis*] of the Spirit into Galilee" (Luke 4:14). This is the baptism of the Spirit.

Exousia: Authority

Exousia means "delegated influence, in the sense of control authority, jurisdiction, power, right, strength."[23] It deals primarily with authority. It was with authority that Jesus healed the sick and cast out demons. There were times however when both *dunamis* and *exousia* were employed.

Jesus said, "All power [*exousia*] is given unto me in heaven and in earth. Go ye therefore" (Matt. 28:18–19). Jesus is saying to us that God has put all authority in heaven and earth into His hands, therefore you go in His authority. When the scriptures speak of going in His name, it is talking about His authority. He has given that to us.

In the gospel of Luke, the Bible gives us an example where both authority and miracle-working power was used by Jesus.

> And they were all amazed, and spake among themselves, saying, What a word is this! for with authority [*exousia*] and power [*dunamis*] he commandeth the unclean spirits, and they come out. (Luke 4:36)

Kratos: Dominion

Kratos means, "force, strength, power, might: mighty with great power, a mighty deed, a work of power, dominion."[24]

Here are two examples of *kratos* in the scripture.

> Finally, my brethren, be strong in the Lord, and in the power (*kratos*) of his might [His ability to hold]. (Eph. 6:10)

> Strengthened with all might (*dunamis*), according to his glorious power (*kratos*), unto all patience and long-suffering with joyfulness. (Col. 1:11)

23. Strong's Hebrew and Greek Dictionaries, s.v. "*exousia,*" 1890, public domain.

24. Strong's Hebrew and Greek Dictionaries, s.v. "*kratos,*" 1890, public domain.

There are three words for power in the New Testament, yet they are all translated using only one English word—*power*. This is why when we are studying the word of God we need to have resources on hand to help us understand. I recommend Strong's Hebrew and Greek dictionaries and Thayer's Greek definitions.

Who Has the Power?

Paul said, "But we have this treasure in earthen vessels, that the excellency of the power [*dunamis*] may be of God, and not of us" (2 Cor. 4:7).

Paul says that we have this treasure in earthen vessels—that is us; our bodies are earthen vessels. The Greek word for *treasure* is *thesaurus*, which means "a deposit in wealth."[25] The treasure he is talking about is *dunamis*, the miracle-working power of God that is deposited in us. He speaks of the excellency of this power. The word *excellency* translated from Greek is the word *huperbole*. It means "to surpass abundance beyond measure."[26]

This superabundant miracle-working power is of God and not of us, but God has placed it in us and we have access to it when needed. Paul told us that " the gifts and calling of God are without repentance" (Rom. 11:29). When God gives you a gift, He doesn't take it back.

The *zoe* life of God Almighty manifested in you in His full and complete power and glory.

The last promise of this prophetic word is the glory of God is manifested in us. I am not sure that I have the words to properly define the glory of God. The following is a definition I think probably only scratches the surface:

> Splendor, brightness; magnificence, excellence, preeminence, dignity, grace; majesty; a thing belonging

---

25. Strong's Hebrew and Greek Dictionaries, s.v. "*thesaurus,*" 1890, public domain.

26. Strong's Hebrew and Greek Dictionaries, s.v. "*huperbole,*" 1890, public domain.

to God; the kingly majesty which belongs to Him as supreme ruler, majesty in the sense of the absolute perfection of the deity;[27]

Remember that David said in the Psalms:

For thou hast made him a little lower than the angels, [*Elohiym*] and hast crowned him with glory and honour.

Thou madest him to have dominion over the works of thy hands; thou hast put all things under his feet. (Ps. 8:6)

If you can receive this, it will change your perspective as to who you really are in the kingdom of God.

King David is saying that *Elohiym*, the creator God, the God who calls things that are not as though they were, has created man like Himself and set him just under Himself. The only thing that is above man is God the Father, God the Son, and God the Holy Spirit. Not only has He set him in this high place, but He crowned him with glory and honor. In the book of John, Jesus said that He sent us into the world, just as the Father sent Him into the world, and furthermore, He sent us with the same glory that the Father sent Him with (see John 17:18, 22). God has given man dominion, rulership, and authority over all the works of His hands.

Paul said in Ephesians 1:12, "That we should be to the praise of his glory, who first trusted in Christ." He has given us all these gifts; He deposited in us this excellent treasure of miracle-working power, not for our glory, but for His. We are to glorify Him, and He has provided every tool we need in order to achieve that goal.

Jesus has endowed us with miraculous spiritual gifts through the baptism of the Holy Spirit so that His glory may shine forth through us,

---

27. Thayer and Smith, "Greek Lexicon entry for *Doxa*," The KJV New Testament Greek Lexicon, accessed November 11, 2020, https://www.biblestudytools.com/lexicons/greek/kjv/doxa.html.

demonstrating His love for the world. All of this will be accomplished through a close intimate relationship with Jesus.

Brothers and sisters, we must not take for granted the love of Jesus Christ. He has provided everything we need to rise to the level necessary to sit on that couch with Him in sweet communion as He shares His secrets with us. Can you not see how He looks right past all our failures, forgiving and cleansing us and making us worthy to sit on that couch with Him? He desires with all His heart to sit on that couch with you, holding you close, loving you and encouraging you and strengthening you making you ready to go forth in His power and His might shining forth His (shekinah) glory to the world.

> But seek ye first the kingdom of God, and his righteousness; and all these things shall be added unto you. (Matt. 6:33)

CHAPTER 8: IMPUTED RIGHTEOUSNESS

And this is His name whereby he shall be called, THE LORD OUR RIGHTEOUSNESS. (Jer. 23:6)

T he culmination of God's covenant, God's *hesed*, and God's salvation is this most precious gift from our heavenly Father, the imputed righteousness of Jesus Christ our Lord and Savior.

In the beginning, God said, "Let us make man in our image, after our likeness: and let them have dominion" (Genesis 1:26). Four thousand years later this was complete in Jesus Christ. Only a loving Father like Him could make a way for us, His rebellious children. We can stand before Him without spot or blemish, side by side with His most perfect Son, equal with Him in rights, privileges, and authority, and holding our head up without shame, knowing we are accepted in the beloved of the kingdom of God.

Angels and other created beings are not governed by the same laws as people. When the angels fell, they fell as individuals. They had no corporate head; therefore, they could not rise and be forgiven. When God created people, He set them into a representative government. As our representative is, so are we. Under the law of substitution, our representative is our substitute.

Paul says in the book of Romans:

> Therefore as by the offence of one judgment came upon all men to condemnation; even so by the righteousness of one the free gift came upon all men unto justification

of life. For as by one man's disobedience many were made sinners, so by the obedience of one shall many be made righteous. (Rom. 5:18–19)

When our representative (Adam) sinned, that sin nature was imputed to us. When we received Jesus as our Lord and Savior, He became our representative, or our substitute. Jesus was without sin. He was perfect without spot or blemish. His nature was perfection in holiness and righteousness. Therefore, since we are exactly like our representative (our substitute), His immaculate righteousness was imputed to us.

> Herein is our love made perfect, that we may have boldness in the day of judgment: because as he is, so are we in this world. (1 John 4:17)

As by representation we fell, it is by the representative system that we rise. The angels fell personally and individually, and they never rise. But we fell in another, and we have therefore the power given by divine grace to rise in another. When we received Jesus as our Lord and Savior, we fell in Him: "I am crucified with Christ" (Gal. 2:20). As He is, so are we. We have been raised together with Him (see Eph. 2:6).

Charles Hodge says it this way in his book *Systematic Theology*:

> When you impute goodness to a man, you do not make him good. So, when righteousness is imputed to the believer, he does not thereby become subjectively righteous. If the righteousness is adequate; and if the imputation is made on adequate grounds; and by a competent authority, the person to whom the imputation is made has the right to be treated as righteous. And, therefore, in the forensic, although not in the moral or subjective sense, the imputation of the righteousness of Christ does make the sinner righteous. That is, it gives him a right to the full pardon of all his sins and a claim in justice to eternal life.[28]

---

28. Charles Hodge, *Systematic Theology Vol. III*, (Thomas Nelson and Sons: New York, 1873), 145.

Two very distinct events took place during these three days of crucifixion. A new covenant was established, and "the Lamb that was slain from before the foundation of the world" was sacrificed to take away the sin of the world, making available to us the spotless white robe of the righteousness of Jesus Christ.

Establishing the New Covenant

First, there is a ceremony establishing the new covenant with God and man. This can be found in Matthew, Mark, and Luke. We will look at Matthew. Then it must be consummated with the shedding of blood.

> And as they were eating, Jesus took bread, and blessed it, and brake it, and gave it to the disciples, and said, Take, eat; this is my body. And he took the cup, and gave thanks, and gave it to them, saying, Drink ye all of it; For this is my blood of the new testament, which is shed for many for the remission of sins. But I say unto you, I will not drink henceforth of this fruit of the vine, until that day when I drink it new with you in my Father's kingdom. (Matt. 26:26–29)

The consummation began in the garden of Gethsemane with Jesus sweating great drops of blood.

Jesus's experience in the garden of Gethsemane was of paramount importance to the entire crucifixion event. I believe Jesus would have died right there in the garden if God had not intervened. The garden event was the first challenge that Jesus had to conquer. I have heard many times preachers saying on Easter Sunday that Jesus was just showing His humanity in the garden, trying to get out of the crucifixion. I petitioned the Lord many times to reveal to me the truth of the garden event. I knew in my heart that Jesus was not trying to get out of it.

Was Jesus showing His humanity when He was praying to God, asking Him to remove this cup from Him? Was He truly trying to get out of the crucifixion? We will examine scripture to determine the answer.

> And he went a little further, and fell on his face, and prayed, saying, O my Father, if it be possible, let this cup pass from me: nevertheless not as I will, but as thou wilt. (Matt. 26:39)

> He went away again the second time, and prayed, saying, O my Father, if this cup may not pass away from me, except I drink it, thy will be done. (Matt. 26:42)

> And he left them, and went away again, and prayed the third time, saying the same words. (Matt. 26:44)

I cannot accept the premise that Jesus wanted out of the crucifixion. When someone says that Jesus was just showing His humanity and asking God to get Him out of the crucifixion, I get the impression that Jesus was walking in circles, wringing His hands and whining to God, begging Him to save Him.

Hebrews 11:35-37 says about followers of Christ:

> Others were tortured, not accepting deliverance; that they might obtain a better resurrection: And others had trial of cruel mockings and scourgings, yea, moreover of bonds and imprisonment: They were stoned, they were sawn asunder, were tempted, were slain with the sword: they wandered about in sheepskins and goatskins; being destitute, afflicted, tormented.

Are those who say that Jesus was showing His humanity by wanting to get out of the crucifixion saying that He was weaker than His followers?

No, this doesn't even makes sense! If Jesus, like His followers, wanted out of suffering, all they had to do was deny that Jesus was the Son of God. And thousands did when persecution came. Jesus didn't need God to get Him out of suffering; all He had to do was stand up in the Sanhedrin court and deny Himself.

CHAPTER 8: IMPUTED RIGHTEOUSNESS

I cannot accept this description of Our Lord and Savior Jesus Christ. Even when I didn't know anything about the Word of God I had read enough Bible to know that this could not possibly be a picture of Jesus. Let me show you some scriptures that describes Jesus the way He really is.

> And all that dwell upon the earth shall worship him, whose names are not written in the book of life of the Lamb slain from the foundation of the world. (Rev. 13:8)

It was predetermined that Jesus would have to die to pay for the sin of the whole world even before the world was created.

> Looking unto Jesus the author and finisher of our faith; who for the joy that was set before him endured the cross, despising the shame, and is set down at the right hand of the throne of God. (Heb. 12:2)

The writer of Hebrews said that it was with joy that Jesus looked forward to enduring the cross.

> From that time forth began Jesus to shew unto his disciples, how that he must go unto Jerusalem, and suffer many things of the elders and chief priests and scribes, and be killed, and be raised again the third day. (Matt. 16:21)

Jesus knew for years that He was to be scourged and crucified by the Romans. This was His plan from before the foundation of the world. In the book of Philippians, Paul shows us the mind of Christ.

> Let this mind be in you, which was also in Christ Jesus: Who, being in the form of God, thought it not robbery to be equal with God: But made himself of no reputation, and took upon him the form of a servant, and was made in the likeness of men: And being found in fashion as

95

a man, he humbled himself, and became obedient unto death, even the death of the cross (Phil. 2:5–8).

When you read these scriptures that describe Jesus's knowledge of coming events pertaining to the cross and His attitude about going to the cross, how can you believe that He was trying to get out of the crucifixion?

When you interpret scripture, you have to interpret scripture with scripture. You can't take one set of scripture and make a doctrine without other scripture agreeing with it. There is no other scripture in the Bible that even remotely suggests that Jesus did not want to go to the cross.

Jesus was the Lamb of God. He was the only one who could be the sacrificial Lamb. There is a whole lot more to that statement, but that is not the subject of this teaching, suffice it to say that if Jesus had not gone to the cross, we would still be in our sins and without hope.

Certainly, there was something going on with Jesus for Him to pray that prayer asking God if this cup could pass from Him. He did need a cup to pass, but the cup He was referring to was not the crucifixion.

Jesus was under extreme pressure. We know this because the Bible says, "And being in an agony he prayed more earnestly: and his sweat was as it were great drops of blood falling down to the ground" (Luke 22:44). Jesus was literally sweating blood.

There is a phenomenon known as hematidrosis. Hematidrosis occurs when the body and mind are under extreme pressure and will cause the capillaries to open up and secrete blood into the sweat glands and the person will literally sweat blood.

Luke says that He was in agony. The word *agony* is translated from the Greek word *agonia. Agonia* means "of severe mental struggles and emotions, agony, anguish."[29]

---

29. Thayer and Smith, "Greek Lexicon entry for *Agonia*," The KJV New Testament Greek Lexicon", accessed November 11, 2020, https://www.biblestudytools.com/lexicons/greek/kjv/agonia.html.

CHAPTER 8: IMPUTED RIGHTEOUSNESS

Jesus was certainly suffering great mental anguish, but what was causing it? I could not accept that Jesus was trying to get out of the cross, there had to be something else going on. I went to the Lord many times asking Him to show me what was happening with Jesus there in the garden. I reminded the Holy Spirit that Jesus promised us that He would lead us into all truth. Finally one Sunday morning the Lord showed me what was happening to Jesus that caused all that torment.

I was ministering, and after I had preached a woman brought her grown daughter up for prayer. The daughter seemed to be in her mid-thirties and you could tell from the daughter's appearance that she had lived a hard life. I found out later that she had been living on the streets. She was addicted to drugs and had done whatever was needed to get the drugs. She was a prostitute and a thief. There was nothing she wouldn't do to get her next fix.

When it came time for me to pray for her, I stood in front of her and waited for the Holy Spirit to tell me how to pray for her. The Holy Spirit told me to hug her. I thought that the Holy Spirit was going to impart His Spirit into her and deliver her, but that's not what happened. As I got close to her to put my arms around her, the most horrible feeling came onto me. I really can't explain what it was. It was like there was a filthy aurora around her. It literally made my skin crawl and tingle. It was so filthy and nasty I couldn't stand it and I had to get away from her. It was so awful I don't have the words to describe it.

As I was walking away from her the Holy Spirit spoke to me and said, "What you were experiencing is sin. This is what was happening to Jesus in the garden."

Jesus had never experienced sin. His body was pure and without sin, therefore when God started to put the sin of the world on to Jesus, it was a tremendous shock to His body.

What I experienced was just a sample of the sin of one person, and that was repulsive to me. In our everyday life, we don't notice the sin that we are exposed to because we have experienced it all our life. Jesus had never experienced sin before. Even if He had, no human body could carry the sin of the world.

The Lord revealed to me that it was the result of receiving sin into His body, not the fear of suffering, that made Him sweat blood.

Jesus had not only become the sacrificial lamb, but the scapegoat for the world's sins. Just as the high priest would lay his hands on the scapegoat for the sins of Israel and transfer all the sin to the scapegoat, God was laying His hands on Jesus and transferring the sins of the world to Jesus (see Leviticus 16). Just imagine all the sins from Adam to Jesus and all the sins from Jesus to the last man laid upon one man. That would kill any man if God did that today. It is no wonder that Jesus was sweating great drops of blood! I believe that Jesus knew He was going to die right there in the garden and never make it to the cross if God did not remove this cup from Him.

> And there appeared an angel unto him from heaven, strengthening him. (Luke 22:43)

This is what Jesus was praying for. He needed strength from heaven— supernatural strength—if He was going to be able to finish His mission.

This happened only one other time in Jesus's life. When He went into the wilderness and fasted forty days God had to send angels to minister to Him. He had to have supernatural strength to be able to fast forty days.

> Then the devil leaveth him, and, behold, angels came and ministered unto him. (Matt. 4:11)

Jesus was focused on the cross. He knew He had to finish the mission. Nothing less would do. It was the only way to certify the new covenant and to establish the New Testament church, the church of Jesus Christ.

> Now is my soul troubled; and what shall I say? Father, save me from this hour: but for this cause came I unto this hour. (John 12:27)

This is why He was here. "But for this cause came I unto this hour."

Thank you, Jesus!

Now that God had sent an angel to strengthen Jesus, He was ready to begin to take away the sin of the whole world.

At this point, our redemption had begun.

The consummation of the covenant continued with much more shedding of blood by Jesus as they beat Him and nailed Him to the cross. The final blow was the piercing of His side with the spear. He was already dead when this happened, but it was the last of the shedding of blood.

What was the significance of Jesus going to the cross? Jesus had to take on Himself not only all of our sins, but He also had to take on Him the curse of the covenant according to covenant law. When the covenant is broken, the covenant breaker must die. So Jesus took our curse on Himself.

> Christ hath redeemed us from the curse of the law, being made a curse for us: for it is written, Cursed is every one that hangeth on a tree. (Gal. 3:13)

Jesus was the sacrificial Lamb that took away the sin of the world. The Lamb that was slain from before the foundation of the world.

"It is finished," He said and gave up the ghost (John 19:30). "Father, into Thy hands I commend my spirit" (Luke 23:46). At that moment all the sacrifices are made complete. Jesus was the sacrificial Lamb.

In his writings, Horatius Bonar gives us very detailed and crucial information about the different offerings and elements involved with giving offerings that I believe help us make a better connection with what Jesus sacrificed.

> This perfection or consummation proclaims to us such things as these: the completion of the Father's purpose, the completion of atonement, the completion of the justifying work, the complete-ness of the sin-bearing and law-fulfilling, the completeness of the righteousness, the completeness of the covenant and the covenant seal. All is done, and done by Him who is Son of man and Son of God; perfectly and for ever done; nothing to be added to it or taken from it, by man, by Satan, or by God.

> The moment Jesus gave up the ghost, the gavel came down and you were declared innocent.[30]

> The old burnt-offering of the patriarchs, on the footing of which these fathers had in ages past drawn near to God, was split into many parts; and in the details of these we see the fulness and variety of the substitution.

> The various sacrifices are well connected with the altar; and even that which was "burnt without the camp" was connected with the altar. It was no doubt carried forth without the camp, and burnt with fire (Lev 6:30, 16:27); but "the blood was brought into the tabernacle of the congregation, to reconcile withal in the holy place." "The blood of the bullock was brought in, to make atonement in the holy place." Their connection with the altar is sufficient of itself to show the truth of substitution contained in them, for the altar was the place of transference. But in each of them we find something which expresses this more directly and fully.

---

30. The Everlasting Righteousness; Or, How Shall Man Be Just with God? by Horatius Bonar, chapter 4.

In the *burnt-offering* we see the perfection of the substitute presented in the room of our imperfection, in not loving God with our whole heart.

In the *meat-offering* we have the perfection of the substitute, as that on which, when laid upon the altar, God feeds, and on which He invites us to feed.

In the *peace-offering* we find the perfection of the substitute laid on the same altar as an atonement, reconciling us to God; removing the distance and the enmity, and providing food for us out of that which had passed through death; for "He is our peace."

In the *sin-offering* we see the perfection of the substitute, whose blood is sprinkled on the altar, and whose body is burnt without, as securing pardon for unconscious sins,-sins of ignorance.

In the *trespass-offering* there is the same perfection of the substitute, in His atoning character, procuring forgiveness for conscious and willful sin.

In the *drink-offering* we have the perfection of the substitute poured out on the altar, as that by which God is refreshed, and by which we are also refreshed. "His blood is drink indeed."

In the *incense* we have the "sweet savor" of the substitute going up to God in our behalf, the cloud of fragrance from His life and death with which God is well pleased, enveloping us and making us fragrant with a fragrance not our own; absorbing all in us that is displeasing or hateful, and replacing it with a sweetness altogether perfect and divine.

In the *fire* we see the holy wrath of the Judge consuming the victim slain in the sinner's room. In the ashes we have the proof that the wrath had spent itself, that the penalty was paid, that the work was done. "It is finished," was the voice of the ashes on the altar.

In all this we see such things as the following: (1) God's displeasure against sin; (2) that displeasure exhausted in a righteous way; (3) the substitute presented and accepted; (4) the substitute slain and consumed; (5) the transference of the wrath from the sinner to his representative; (6) God resting in His love over the sinner, and viewing him in the perfection of his substitute; (7) the sinner reconciled, accepted, complete, enjoying God's favour, and feeding at His table on that on which God had fed; on that which had come from the altar, and had passed through the fire.[31]

Charles Spurgeon spoke on this topic as well, and had a lot to say about Jesus as the Lord our Righteousness. It is so important for us to understand Jesus in that light before we can take it to the next step.

I think we may take it thus: When we believe in Christ, by faith we receive our justification. As the merit of His blood takes away our sin, so the merit of His obedience is imputed to us for righteousness. We are considered, as soon as we believe, as though the works of Christ were our works. God looks upon us as though that perfect obedience, of which I have just now spoken, had been performed by ourselves. God considers us as though we were Christ—looks upon us as though His life had been our life—and accepts, blesses, and rewards

31. Horatius Bonar, The Everlasting Righteousness; or, How Shall Man Be Just with God?, (James Nisbet and Co.: London, 1873), 21.

us as though all that He did had been done by us, His believing people.[32]

And now let us stop a moment and think over this whole title—"The Lord our righteousness." Brethren, the Law-giver has himself obeyed the law Do you not think that his obedience will be sufficient? Jehovah has himself become man that so he may do man's work: think you that he has done it imperfectly? Jehovah—he who girds the angels that excel in strength—has taken upon him the form of a servant that he may become obedient: think you that his service will be incomplete? Let the fact that the Saviour is Jehovah strengthen your confidence. Be ye bold. Be ye very courageous. Face heaven, and earth, and hell with the challenge of the apostle. "Who shall say anything to the charge of God's elect? "Look back upon your past sins, look upon your present infirmities, and all your future errors, and while you weep the tears of repentance, let no fear of damnation blanch your cheek. You stand before God to-day robed in your Saviour's garments, "with his spotless vestments on, holy as the Holy One." Not Adam when he walked in Eden's bowers was more accepted than you are,—not more pleasing to the eye of the all-judging, the sin-hating God than you are if clothed in Jesus' righteousness and sprinkled with his blood. You have a better righteousness than Adam had. He had a human righteousness; your garments are divine. He had a robe complete, it is true, but the earth had woven it. You have a garment as complete, but heaven has made it for you to wear. Go up and down in the strength of this great truth and boast exceedingly, and glory in your

32. Jehovah Tsidkenu: The Lord Our Righteousness, A Sermon (No. 395) Delivered on Sunday Morning, June 2nd, 1861 by the Rev. C. H. SPURGEON, At the Metropolitan Tabernacle, Newington.

God; and let this be on the top and summit of your heart and soul: "Jehovah, the Lord our righteousness."[33]

After we see Jesus as the Lord our Righteousness, then naturally we can see how the righteousness of Christ is imputed to the believer for his justification. Look at what some earlier theologians have to say about this process.

> This does not, and cannot mean that the righteousness of Christ is infused into the believer or in any way so imparted to him as to change, or constitute His moral character. Imputation never changes the inward, subjective state of the person to whom the imputation is made. . . . It gives him a right to the full pardon of all his sins and a claim in justice to eternal life.

> The law is not completely fulfilled by the endurance of penalty only. It must also be obeyed. Christ both endured the penalty due to man for disobedience, and perfectly obeyed the law for him; so that He was a vicarious substitute in reference to both the precept and the penalty of the law. By his active obedience He obeyed the law, and by his passive obedience He endured the penalty. In this way his vicarious work is complete.[34]

> Christ may be said to be the end of the Law because the end of the Law is perfect righteousness, that a man may be justified thereby, which end we cannot attain of ourselves through the frailty of our flesh. But by Christ we attain it, Who hath fulfilled the Law for us. Christ hath perfectly fulfilled the Decalogue for us and that three ways: (1.) in His pure conception; (2.) in His godly life; and (3.) in His holy and obedient sufferings and all for us. For

---

33. Jehovah Tsidkenu: The Lord Our Righteousness, A Sermon (No. 395) Delivered on Sunday Morning, June 2nd, 1861 by the Rev. C. H. SPURGEON, At the Metropolitan Tabernacle, Newington.

34. Charles Hodge, *Systematic Theology, vol. 3*, (Charles Scribner;s Sons: New York, 1895), 106.

whatsoever the Law required that we should be, do, or suffer, He hath performed in our behalf. We are discharged by Him before God…

The infinite wisdom and power of dear Jesus in reconciling the Law and the Gospel in this great mystery of justification is greatly to be magnified. This righteousness presents us in the sight of God as "all fair" (Song 4:7); as "complete" (Colossians 2:10); as "without spot or wrinkle" (Ephesians 5:27); as "without fault before the throne of God" (Revelation 14:5); as "holy, and unblameable, and unreproveable in his sight" (Colossians 1:22).[35]

Can you now see yourselves standing in freedom and glory clothed in the precious white robes of Jesus Christ, with God Almighty looking upon you as righteous as His Son? What a beautiful picture this is, and something that we can easily take for granted as the born-again believer. Horatius Bonar gave us a great summation of this truth:

"Their righteousness is of ME, saith the Lord" (Isa. 54:17); for "He, of God, is made unto righteousness" (1 Cor. 1:30). The transference is complete and eternal. From the moment that we receive the divine testimony to the righteousness of the Son of God, all the guilt that was on us passes over to Him, and all His righteousness passes over to us; so that God looks on us as possessed of that righteousness, and treats us according to its value in His sight.[36]

"The Lord our Righteousness" is His name. As the bride of Christ, it is now our name. We are the righteousness of God Almighty, and we stand before Him righteous. When God looks at us He sees us standing there wearing white robes of righteousness that was provided by Jesus Himself.

---

35. Rev. Thomas Brooks, *The Golden Key to Open Hidden Treasures*, (1675, public domain).

36. Horatius Bonar, The Everlasting Righteousness; or, How Shall Man Be Just with God?, (James Nisbet and Co.: London, 1873), 71.

God does not see past those robes. He is not looking at the evil of our past lives. He can't see it! He can only see those white robes that are without spot or blemish, shining with that shekinah glory of Jesus, brighter than the sun. We can stand before Him with our heads held high, humble but not in shame. All the shame was taken away by Jesus.

> Herein is our love made perfect, that we may have boldness in the day of judgment: because as he is, so are we in this world. (1 John 4:17)

CHAPTER 9: BAPTISM IN THE HOLY SPIRIT

I t was during the feast of Pentecost when Jesus gave the baptism in the Holy Spirit, establishing His New Testament church. To understand the significance of what took place in this event, we need to go back and look at the original Pentecost to see what happened then and how it relates to this Pentecost. Every year since God had first established the Feast of Pentecost, it has been celebrated. So what was so special about this particular feast?

Fifty days after leaving Egypt, God told Moses to go to the top of Mount Sinai and He would meet him there. When God came down on that mountain, He was announced by the blowing of the trumpet by ten thousands of angels.

> And he said, The LORD came from Sinai, and rose up from
> Seir unto them; he shined forth from mount Paran, and he
> came with ten thousands of saints: from his right hand went
> a fiery law for them. (Deut. 33:2)

On top of Mount Sinai, God met with Moses for forty days and gave to him the laws and ordinances. They were to govern God's chosen people, and in so doing, God entered into a covenant with Israel.

I want to stop here and point something out that we should not forget. God entered into a covenant with His chosen people—which was all of Israel, not just the Jews. There were twelve tribes in Israel; the tribe of Judah was only one tribe of the twelve. His covenant with the twelve tribes of Israel is still in force. His chosen people are all twelve tribes, not just the Jews.

After forty days, Moses came down from the mountain and found that the people had become impatient and talked Aaron into making them an idol to worship. He had the ringleaders killed, which were about three thousand people.

On the fiftieth day after the first Passover, God entered into a covenant with the nation of Israel and established the church in the wilderness.

Now let us fast forward to the Feast of Pentecost, which was fifty days after Jesus's resurrection.

This Feast of Pentecost would be different than any other Feast of Pentecost, since the original was where God met Moses on top of Mount Sinai.

Jesus had told His disciples to go to Jerusalem and wait for the promise.

> And, being assembled together with them, commanded them that they should not depart from Jerusalem, but wait for the promise of the Father, which, saith he, ye have heard of me.
>
> For John truly baptized with water; but ye shall be baptized with the Holy Ghost not many days hence. (Acts 1:4–5)

It is important to remember that according to the custom of the Jews, the day began at sunset and ended at the next sunset. Therefore, the Feast of Pentecost began at sunset at the beginning of the fiftieth day after the Feast of Firstfruits which was the day Jesus was resurrected from the dead. Jesus, of course, being the Firstfruits of many sons, as Paul said to the Corinthians: "But now is Christ risen from the dead, and become the firstfruits of them that slept" (1 Corinthians 15:20).

It was their custom to celebrate the Feast of Pentecost by staying up all night reading scripture, praying, and singing hymns and praising God. It was about nine in the morning when they were all in the upper room and they heard a sound.

> And when the day of Pentecost was fully come, they were
> all with one accord in one place. And suddenly there came a
> sound from heaven as of a rushing mighty wind, and it filled
> all the house where they were sitting. (Act 2:1–2)

I have often wondered what that sound was that they heard. It had to be very loud because it was heard not just in that upper room, but all over Jerusalem. We know that because the scripture tells about it: "Now when this was noised abroad, the multitude came together" (Acts 2:6).

In Greek the words, "noised abroad" literally mean "when the sound was heard." Jerusalem was a very large city. Because of the Feast of Pentecost, there had to be hundreds of thousands of people there. This same noise that the disciples heard in the upper room was heard all over Jerusalem.

We know that God came down that day to the upper room where the disciples were gathered together. We also know from Scripture that when God comes down, He is announced by tens of thousands of angels blowing trumpets. When God came down on Mount Sinai He was announced by tens of thousands of angels blowing trumpets. When Jesus was born, we know that the angels announced His birth to the shepherds.

In the first event on Mount Sinai, God established His church in the wilderness. In the second event, God announced the birth of our redeemer. In this third event, God has come down again to establish the New Testament church of Jesus Christ.

I believe the sound that Dr. Luke described as a sound of a mighty rushing wind was the sound of tens of thousands of angels blowing tens of thousands of angel-size trumpets.

God came down that day and baptized those one hundred and twenty disciples in the Holy Ghost and fire (see Acts 2:3–4). Jesus had already initiated the twelve apostles into the new covenant on the night that they celebrated the Passover just before His crucifixion (see Luke 22:20). Jesus is the Baptizer in the Holy Spirit. In baptizing these one hundred and twenty, He established His New Testament church.

Immediately they all began to speak in unknown tongues, and under a heavy influence of the Holy Spirit, they poured out onto the street. With boldness, Peter began to preach, and three thousand were saved and added to the church that day (see Acts 2:41).

The disciples had obeyed Jesus, waiting in Jerusalem to receive the promise of the Holy Spirit (see Acts 1:8). Now they were equipped to begin their ministry.

Jesus said that you would receive power after the Holy Ghost has come upon you. Remember that the Greek word for *power* here is *dunamis*— miracle-working power. He is saying to us, "Don't start your ministry, don't teach Sunday school, don't clean the church, don't do anything until you are equipped with the baptism in the Holy Spirit." Jesus said, "You need this miracle-working power to be a witness of Me."

Jesus commanded the disciples to wait for the promise. The baptism in the Holy Spirit is not an optional add-on if you want it for your ministry; Jesus commands us to get it. It is an essential tool that we need to be a proper witness for Jesus.

The Greek word for *witness* is *martus*, which means "evidence producer." That is what a witness does—they present evidence. We are to be "evidence producers" everywhere we go. Jesus said to go into all the world and preach the gospel, lay hands on the sick, speak in unknown tongues, and cast out demons (see Mark 16:15–18). Once we are baptized in the Holy Spirit, we are equipped to obey Jesus.

The unique difference between the establishment of the church in the wilderness and the establishment of the New Testament church is the baptism in the Holy Spirit with the initial evidence of speaking in tongues. Nine gifts of the Spirit come with the baptism in the Holy Spirit. Of these nine gifts, only two are not found in the Old Testament church, and those are the gifts of tongues and the interpretation of tongues. The gift of tongues is the unique gift of the baptism of the Holy Spirit.

Jesus commanded us to be baptized in the Holy Spirit so that we would be endued with power from on high. Jesus Himself was baptized in the Holy Spirit. He laid down His deity when He came to the earth and therefore, He functioned on the earth as a man (see Phil. 2:5–7).

Jesus commanded that we be baptized in water and in the Holy Spirit, just like He was before He began His ministry (see Mark 1:9–11). Operating as a man in the earth, He had to be endued with power from on high before He could begin His ministry. The scriptures do not record a single miracle done by Jesus before He was baptized in the Holy Spirit.

Jesus had done everything a devoted Jew was supposed to do. He was well trained in the scriptures. He could quote the first five books of the Bible by heart, but He still lacked one thing—and that was the baptism in the Holy Spirit. He had to receive power from on high. He had to be highly anointed by God to fulfill His ministry. He would be severely tested throughout His ministry and He would not be able to pass the test without the power of the Holy Spirit (see Mark 1:12–13).

Just as Jesus had to have the power of the Holy Spirit working through Him, we also must have the Holy Spirit working through us to overcome the power of the enemy. There are many reasons we need the baptism of the Holy Spirit to endue us with power from on high. One of the most important reasons is that the baptism of the Holy Spirit is the gateway into the nine manifestation gifts of the Spirit. These are all gifts that we will use throughout our ministry. The gift of tongues is very important to us because it is through this gift that we receive power to strengthen our spirit, increasing our ability to hear the Spirit of God.

Evidence of Baptism in the Holy Spirit: Tongues

Some people teach that you can be baptized in the Holy Spirit and not speak in tongues, but that is not what Scripture teaches. These teachers always go to 1 Corinthians 12:30 where Paul is asking a question making a point in his teaching:

Have all the gifts of healing? Do all speak with tongues? Do
all interpret? (1 Cor. 12:30)

They look at that scripture and say this is proof that Paul is saying that
everybody doesn't speak in tongues. This is taking the scripture out of context.
In this context, Paul is talking about the gifts of administrations. Tongues
with the interpretation of tongues is one of the gifts of administrations. Paul
is simply saying that everyone does not have a gift of administration, but
everyone does receive their own personal prayer language, "tongues."

The Bible teaches by example as well as through precept. There are five
examples in the book of Acts that demonstrate that everyone who receives
the baptism in the Holy Spirit does speak in an unknown tongue. The first
example that we will look at is on the day of Pentecost when the hundred
and twenty were together in one accord in the upper room. The book of Acts
says that "they were *all* filled with the Holy Ghost, and began to speak with
other tongues" (Acts 2:4). They were baptized in the Holy Spirit, therefore
they spoke in tongues.

The second example is at the Samaritan Revival. Acts 8:4–25 tells the
account of Phillip going down to Samaria to preach the gospel of Jesus
Christ. As Phillip was preaching and teaching the word of God; many were
saved, healed, and delivered with many miracles being performed. The
scripture says that there was great joy in that city because of this revival.

There was a sorcerer there named Simon who also believed and was
saved. When the apostles at Jerusalem heard about this great revival, they
sent John and Peter to Samaria. When they got there, they found that the
people had been saved and water baptized, but had not received the baptism
in the Holy Spirit (see Acts 8:15–17). The scripture does not specifically say
that they spoke in tongues after they were baptized in the Holy Spirit, but
it strongly implies that there was certainly something different about them.

> And when Simon saw that through laying on of the
> apostles' hands the Holy Ghost was given, he offered them
> money, saying, give me also this power, that on whomsoever
> I lay hands, he may receive the Holy Ghost.

What did Simon see that was different? He had already seen everyone baptized in water. He had already seen great miracles. He had already seen unclean spirits cast out, and all this before Peter and John came to town. So what did he see that made him want to be able to do what the apostles had done? The only thing it could be would be speaking in tongues.

For the third example, we will go to the ninth chapter of Acts and look at Paul's experience of being baptized in the Holy Spirit. In this account, Paul (Saul) is on his way to Damascus to arrest Christians when Jesus meets him on the road, blinds him, and then tells him to go to Damascus and wait for further instructions. Jesus then sends Ananias to open his eyes and get him saved and baptized in the Holy Spirit. In Paul's case, he is saved and filled with the Spirit before he is water baptized.

> And Ananias went his way, and entered into the house; and putting his hands on him said, Brother Saul, the Lord, even Jesus, that appeared unto thee in the way as thou camest, hath sent me, that thou mightest receive thy sight, and be filled with the Holy Ghost. And immediately there fell from his eyes as it had been scales: and he received sight forthwith, and arose, and was baptized.

Again in these scriptures, it does not say specifically that Paul spoke in tongues, but we know that Paul did speak in tongues. In 1 Corinthians, he says, "I thank my God, I speak with tongues more than ye all" (1 Corinthians 14:18). So if he did not speak in tongues when he received the baptism in the Holy Spirit, when did he begin to speak in tongues?

The fourth example of speaking in tongues after receiving the baptism in the Holy Spirit is found in Acts 10. For the first time in Scripture, God is sending Peter to the house of a Gentile to preach the gospel of Jesus Christ. It took some convincing for Peter to accept this assignment since it was considered unlawful for an Israelite to enter a Gentile's house. Gentiles were considered unclean.

> There was a certain man in Caesarea called Cornelius, a centurion of the band called the Italian band, a devout

man, and one that feared God with all his house, which gave much alms to the people, and prayed to God always. He saw in a vision evidently about the ninth hour of the day an angel of God coming into him and saying unto him, Cornelius. And when he looked on him, he was afraid, and said, What is it, Lord? And he said unto him, Thy prayers and thine alms are come up for a memorial before God. and now send men to Joppa, and call for one Simon, whose surname is Peter. (Acts 10:1-5)

In obedience to God, Peter took brethren and went to Caesarea. Entering Cornelius' house, Peter began to preach the gospel of Jesus Christ to those in the house.

While Peter yet spoke these words, the Holy Ghost fell on all them which heard the word. And they of the circumcision which believed were astonished, as many as came with Peter, because that on the Gentiles also was poured out the gift of the Holy Ghost. For they heard them speak with tongues, and magnify God. Then answered Peter, can any man forbid water, that these should not be baptized, which have received the Holy Ghost as well as we? And he commanded them to be baptized in the name of the Lord. (Acts 10:44-48)

Once again, here is an example where the people were baptized in the Holy Spirit and spoke in tongues before they were water baptized. Dr. Luke, in writing about this event, said that they knew that they were baptized in the Holy Spirit because they heard them speak in tongues. Speaking in an unknown tongue is the initial evidence of being baptized in the Holy Spirit.

In the fifth example, Paul met twelve guys who were saved under the ministry of John the Baptist. Paul then water baptized them in the name of Jesus and then laid hands on them to receive the baptism of the Holy Spirit and they spoke in tongues.

And it came to pass, that, while Apollos was at Corinth, Paul having passed through the upper coasts came to Ephesus: and finding certain disciples, he said unto them, have ye received the Holy Ghost since ye believed? And they said unto him, we have not so much as heard whether there be any Holy Ghost. And he said unto them, unto what then were ye baptized? And they said, Unto John's baptism. Then said Paul, John verily baptized with the baptism of repentance, saying unto the people, that they should believe on him which should come after him, that is, on Christ Jesus. When they heard this, they were baptized in the name of the Lord Jesus. And when Paul had laid his hands upon them, the Holy Ghost came on them; and they spoke with tongues, and prophesied. And all the men were about twelve. (Acts 19:1-7)

These examples taken from Scripture should be sufficient evidence to convince any reasonable person that speaking in an unknown tongue is the initial evidence of the baptism of the Holy Spirit.

Reasons to Pray in Tongues

As I have said, there are many reasons to pray in an unknown tongue. I will give you a few examples from scripture.

Tongues are one of the signs which Jesus declared would follow those that believe: " And these signs shall follow them that believe; in my name shall they cast out devils; they shall speak with new tongues" (Mark 16:17).

Paul teaches us to pray in the Spirit when we don't know how to pray:

Likewise the Spirit also helpeth our infirmities: for we know not what we should pray for as we ought: but the Spirit itself maketh intercession for us with groanings which cannot be uttered. (Rom. 8:26)

Paul teaches us that when we speak in an unknown tongue, we speak directly to God and not to men. When we speak in an unknown tongue, we speak from our spirit to God, bypassing our mind. We don't know what we are saying because it is the Spirit of God praying through our spirit to God. We are praying the perfect will of God. Since it doesn't go through our mind, we can't speak it out, therefore the devil doesn't know what is being prayed. Also, Paul taught that when we pray in tongues, we edify our self:

> For he that speaketh in an unknown tongue speaketh not unto men, but unto God: for no man understandeth him; howbeit in the spirit he speaketh mysteries…He that speaketh in an unknown tongue edifieth himself. (1 Cor. 14:2, 4)

Jude said the same thing: "But ye, beloved, building up yourselves on your most holy faith, praying in the Holy Ghost" (Jude 1:20). Tongues is a means of staying continually filled with the Holy Spirit.

Paul said to pray without ceasing (see 1 Thess. 5:17). The only way you can do that is to pray in the Spirit, which is praying in tongues.

The more you pray in tongues, the more you build up your spirit. The more you build up your spirit, the stronger you are in the Spirit realm. The stronger you are in the Spirit realm, the more you will be able to hear what the Spirit is saying. Therefore, praying in tongues will put you in a position of being able to obey God. The better you hear and obey God, the more He will use you in the greater realms of the Spirit.

It has been my experience after talking with the people of God who are baptized in the Holy Spirit and who speak in tongues, that they invest very little time praying in tongues. It is amazing to me that the most powerful ministry tool that Jesus has given to the church is hardly ever perfected in their lives. At the same time, they complain that they are not seeing what Jesus said we would do in the church, as written in Matthew 10:8: "Heal the sick, cleanse the lepers, raise the dead, cast out devils: freely ye have received, freely give."

Jesus did say that we were to do that, but He also said, " And these signs shall follow them that believe; in my name shall they cast out devils; they shall speak with new tongues" (Mark 16:17). We are expected to perfect the tools God gave us to accomplish the work. Many Christians live a carnal Christian life, never building themselves up in the Spirit and perfecting a relationship with the Holy Spirit. Then they end up disappointed with God when they have no power to deal with a crisis when it comes.

We have been given all the power tools we need to keep the devil in his place and defeat him when he rears his ugly head. If you don't know how to use the tools, you will be defeated. It would be like your neighbor coming to you and saying that an enemy is coming to his house tomorrow to kill him and his family and burn his house down. So you give him an AR-15 and 1,000 rounds of ammunition, and you say to him, "Take this and defend yourself." The next day you see his house burning down.

You ask the man's brother, "What happened?" You tell him that you had given him an AR-15 and 1,000 rounds of ammunition, which should have been all he needed to defend himself. Yet he died and his house was burned down. Then his brother tells you that he didn't know anything about ARs. Here you have a man who has all he needed to defend himself, but he didn't know how to load an AR; he didn't know how to jack a round into the chamber and shoot the gun. He didn't know how to load a magazine or change the magazine in the gun. He had a powerful tool to accomplish the task, but he had no knowledge of the tool, therefore it was useless to him and he was defeated.

Unfortunately, this is a picture of many in the church today. They are surrounded by many powerful tools, but have no clue how to use them. Instead, they depend on the pastor, expecting him to protect them while they do nothing to protect themselves.

I had the privilege of sitting under a great teacher of the Word for a season who told me of a woman who came to church usually only when she needed healing. She would get in the healing line and he would lay hands on her and pray and she would be healed. This went on for several years, always with the same result. Then one Sunday she came to church and got in the healing line, but this time when he prayed for her, she did not get healed. She left the church and told people all over the community that the pastor had lost his anointing. The pastor did not lose his anointing. He is still a highly anointed man of God today. At some point in your life, God expects you to stand on your own anointing. He has given everyone the same measure of faith—and He expects you to perfect it!

> For I say, through the grace given unto me, to every man that is among you, not to think of himself more highly than he ought to think; but to think soberly, according as God hath dealt to every man the measure of faith. (Rom. 12:3)

The more you pray in tongues, the greater your spirit is tuned to God. Your spirit must be perfected to hear that still, small voice that God speaks in. The greatest miracles that God has given me personally, or the times God has used me to give great miracles to someone else, was when He spoke to me instructions in that still, small voice. Had my spirit not been tuned to hear God, I would not have heard Him, and the miracles would not have happened.

What breaks my heart is when God gives me instructions for someone else, and they don't obey God and don't get their miracle. It is usually something very simple, but they just don't believe. It reminds me of when Naaman went to Elisha to be healed. Elisha didn't do it the way Naaman thought it should be done, so he rejected what Elisha told him (see 2 Kings 5:9–14). Naaman was finally convinced by his servant to obey Elisha and was healed. Had he not obeyed Elisha he would never have been healed.

When God gives instructions like this, you have a short window of opportunity to obey God. If you put it off you can't come back and do it later. The window will close.

I cannot emphasize enough how this gift of the Holy Spirit is vital to your life and ministry. Jesus said to the disciples, "Go to Jerusalem and wait for the promise." Jesus insisted that they do nothing until they had the baptism in the Holy Spirit.

It is one thing to be baptized in the Holy Spirit and another thing altogether to be perfected in the Holy Spirit. This should be our goal. It is when we are perfected in the Holy Spirit that we are most useful in the kingdom of God.

CHAPTER 10: SOWING AND REAPING

Matthew, Mark, and Luke all felt that the parable of the sower was important enough to include in their gospels. Furthermore, Jesus took the time to teach it, so we need to seek after more knowledge and understanding of the subject. We will begin by reading the parable, and then we will get deeper into the study of the principle. You should notice that as Jesus is explaining the parable of the sower He connects it to the parable of the ten talents. By connecting the two parables He is making a strong statement. I will use Matthew's account:

> And the disciples came, and said unto him, Why speakest thou unto them in parables? He answered and said unto them, Because it is given unto you to know the mysteries of the kingdom of heaven, but to them it is not given. For whosoever hath, to him shall be given, and he shall have more abundance: but whosoever hath not, from him shall be taken away even that he hath. Therefore speak I to them in parables: because they seeing see not; and hearing they hear not, neither do they understand. And in them is fulfilled the prophecy of Esaias, which saith, By hearing ye shall hear, and shall not understand; and seeing ye shall see, and shall not perceive: For this people's heart is waxed gross, and their ears are dull of hearing, and their eyes they

have closed; lest at any time they should see with their eyes, and hear with their ears, and should understand with their heart, and should be converted, and I should heal them. But blessed are your eyes, for they see: and your ears, for they hear. For verily I say unto you, That many prophets and righteous men have desired to see those things which ye see, and have not seen them; and to hear those things which ye hear, and have not heard them. (Matt. 13:10-17)

Jesus is saying that the disciples get to know the mysteries of the kingdom, but the others do not. Why? Why not everyone? They cannot know the mysteries of the kingdom because they cannot discern the Word of God.

But the natural man receiveth not the things of the Spirit of God: for they are foolishness unto him: neither can he know them, because they are spiritually discerned. (1 Cor. 2:14)

You discern the things of the Spirit by the Spirit. The carnal man has no relationship with the Spirit of God; therefore, he cannot discern the things of the kingdom.

Jesus has also referred to a principle that says that those who have will get more, and those who don't have, even what they think they have will be taken away. The Pharisees thought they were spiritual, but Jesus said, "Except your righteousness shall exceed the righteousness of the scribes and Pharisees, ye shall in no case enter into the kingdom of heaven" (Matt. 5:20).

Let us look first at what Jesus is saying when He is talking about the mysteries of the kingdom of heaven.

What does He mean by "mysteries"? The word *mysteries* is translated from the Greek word *mustērion*. Thayer's definition is "hidden thing, secret, mystery...confided only to the initiated and not to ordinary mortals."[37]

Only the initiated will be invited into the knowledge of the mysteries of the kingdom of God. Only those who are good ground will be able to receive the seed of the word. Only those who prepare their heart to receive the word. Only those who study, meditate, and seek revelation knowledge will be initiated into the knowledge of the mysteries of the kingdom of God. Only those who are seeking the Lord with all their heart will receive the secrets of God.

I have found that even thirty years after many "churchgoers" were saved, they know little more of the Word than the day they were saved. That's because they are not "good ground." True followers of Jesus do what He said to do. They must take up their cross daily.

> And why call ye me, Lord, Lord, and do not the things which I say? (Luke 6:46)

Only those who are seeking the Lord with all their heart will enter into the secrets of God. The blessings of the kingdom do not just fall on someone because they are saved. They must know the principles that govern the kingdom of God and learn how to walk in them. Remember this, "Everything God does is according to a pattern and based on a principle." Pay attention to what I am teaching, and seek after the things of the kingdom.

> And I say unto you, Ask, and it shall be given you; seek, and ye shall find; knock, and it shall be opened unto you. (Luke 11:9)

Albert Barnes said:

---

37. Thayer and Smith, "Greek Lexicon entry for Musterion," The KJV New Testament Greek Lexicon, accessed November 11, 2020, https://www.biblestudytools.com/lexicons/greek/kjv/musterion.html.

The word "mystery" in the Bible, properly means a thing that is "concealed," or that "has been concealed." It does not mean that the thing was "incomprehensible," or difficult to be understood.

The thing might be "plain" enough if revealed, but it means simply that it "had" not been before made known. Thus the "mysteries of the kingdom" do not mean any doctrines incomprehensible in themselves considered, but simply doctrines about the preaching of the gospel and the establishment of the new kingdom of the Christ, which "had not" been understood, and which were as yet concealed from the great body of the Jews.[38]

These mysteries have been hidden from the beginning of time, but they have not been hidden *from* you, they have been hidden *for* you (see Rom. 16:25 and Eph. 3:9).

Now remember what Jesus is talking about here, He is telling the disciples that they are being initiated into the secret counsel of the kingdom of God, but everyone is not. When Jesus uses the word *mystery*, the disciples know what Jesus is saying. He is implying that only certain people will be initiated into the secret things of the kingdom. Everyone can be, but not everyone will be. Only those with good ground. Everyone had the opportunity, but not everyone took advantage of it. Not everyone prepared their ground to receive the seed.

For whosoever hath, to him shall be given, and he shall have more abundance: but whosoever hath not, from him shall be taken away even that he hath. (Matt. 13:12)

Remember in the parable of the talents (Matthew 25:14–30), the master gave his servants equal opportunity to advance in his kingdom. Two out of three took advantage of the opportunity to advance and one did not. The ones who set their sights above where they were, did good

38. Albert Barnes, *Notes on the Bible*, note from Matthew 13:11, (1834, public domain).

and increased, but the other was not only reprimanded, but was cast out of the kingdom.

This servant was in the kingdom of this king, but he was lazy and unprofitable, therefore the king took even what little he had from him and cast him out of his kingdom. Many servants of God are just like this unprofitable servant. They make many excuses to get out of serving.

The Bible says, "For many are called, but few are chosen" (Matthew 22:14). The question is: will we respond?

Paul says that the Holy Spirit gives these gifts (talents) as He wills: "But all these worketh that one and the selfsame Spirit, dividing to every man severally as he will" (1 Cor. 12:11).

There is going to be an accounting. The Lord will come, the books will be opened, and we will have to give an account of our lives (see Revelation 20:12).

> Every man's work shall be made manifest: for the day shall declare it, because it shall be revealed by fire; and the fire shall try every man's work of what sort it is. If any man's work abide which he hath built thereupon, he shall receive a reward. If any man's work shall be burned, he shall suffer loss: but he himself shall be saved; yet so as by fire. (1 Cor. 3:13–15)

We need to know how the kingdom of God works so we can function and operate in the kingdom. We must build our relationship with the Holy Spirit so we can discern the secret mysteries of the kingdom of God.

> Daniel answered and said, Blessed be the name of God for ever and ever: for wisdom and might are his: And he changeth the times and the seasons: he removeth kings, and setteth up kings: he giveth wisdom unto the wise, and knowledge to them that know understanding: He revealeth the deep and secret things: he knoweth what is in the darkness, and the light dwelleth with him. (Dan. 2:20–22)

Those who have developed their wisdom and knowledge receive more, and those who have not, even what little they have is taken away. We are in the kingdom of God, are we not? Should we not, therefore, be grateful and seek after the things of the kingdom of God? Should that not be our priority?

Jesus said, "The sower soweth the word" (Mark 4:14). What does He mean by that? The Greek word *logos* is translated "word" in this sentence. It is the same word in John 1:1, where it says "In the beginning was the Word, and the Word was with God, and the Word was God." We know that John is talking about Jesus in this scripture. Jesus is more than a man of God; He is life and the light of men, He is full of glory, grace, and truth. He is full of supernatural spiritual power. When John says that the sower sows the "word," he's not talking about generic language. He is saying the sower is sowing the very power of God.

> When any one heareth the word of the kingdom, and understandeth it not, then cometh the wicked one, and catcheth away that which was sown in his heart. This is he which received seed by the wayside. (Matt. 13:19)

In Proverbs we are told, "Wisdom is the principal thing; therefore get wisdom: and with all thy getting get understanding" (Proverbs 4:7). We must have spiritual discernment so that we will have understanding. Otherwise, we will become like one who "received seed by the wayside."

> And these are they likewise which are sown on stony ground; who, when they have heard the word, immediately receive it with gladness; And have no root in themselves, and so endure but for a time: afterward, when affliction or persecution ariseth for the word's sake, immediately they are offended. (Mark 4:16–17)

These are those "would be" Christians. They like the message of Christianity and want to be pardoned for their sins, and for a time they try to live the life that they perceive a Christian lives. But when temptation

124

comes with hard times or trouble comes, they fall away. Christ had no root in their heart, so they fall. That's what *offended* means. They never truly gave their heart to Christ. You can recognize them when you see them, they are in and out, in and out, and they never truly get established.

> And that which fell among thorns are they, which, when they have heard, go forth, and are choked with cares and riches and pleasures of this life, and bring no fruit to perfection. (Luke 8:14)

These hearers of the Word can't get their eyes off the world. Their lust for the things of the world consumes them. They can never make Jesus their priority. Therefore, the Word never has a chance to bring forth fruit.

> But that on the good ground are they, which in an honest and good heart, having heard the word, keep it, and bring forth fruit with patience. (Luke 8:15)

These are those who have truly made Jesus the Lord of their life. He is their priority, and that is what they live for. They treasure the Word and live in it every day.

The Bible speaks of seed sown by the wayside, the seed that was sown on stony ground, the seed that was sown on thorny ground and seed that was sown on good ground. Which one brought forth fruit? Only the good ground.

> Abide in me, and I in you. As the branch cannot bear fruit of itself, except it abide in the vine; no more can ye, except ye abide in me. (John 15:4)

His words must abide in us, and we must be connected to the vine to receive life. That is where our life comes from. We must be constantly receiving life from the vine, which, of course, is the Spirit of God.

> For he that hath, to him shall be given: and he that hath
> not, from him shall be taken even that which he hath.
> (Mark 4:25)

Only one type of ground is in a position to receive anything in the kingdom of God. Jesus is not holding out on the other three. They could repent, receive the word, and become good ground.

In this parable, Mark 4:24 says to take heed "what" you hear, and Luke 8:18 says to take heed "how" you hear. It is very important to be able to hear the Word of God and to discern the Word by the Spirit of God.

The seed sown on the wayside, stony, and thorny ground can't receive the secrets of the kingdom because they have made no preparation to be able to receive. They could; everyone can. Jesus will not withhold any good thing from those that are His. It is not a complicated process, just simply seek the understanding.

> And he said, So is the kingdom of God, as if a man
> should cast seed into the ground; And should sleep, and
> rise night and day, and the seed should spring and grow
> up, he knoweth not how. (Mark 4:26–27)

The kingdom of God works with good ground. You don't have to be the most intelligent person in church to know and understand the Word of God. All you must do is humbly receive, believe, and meditate on the Word—and it will grow all by itself in your spirit! Jesus said that it will grow itself. It is like a grain of mustard seed; in time it will become great.

> Be not deceived; God is not mocked: for whatsoever a
> man soweth, that shall he also reap. (Gal. 6:7)

When the Word of God is sown by an anointed man or woman of God, the awesome power of God is released. In Mark 4:14, Jesus says that the sower soweth the Word. The word *sower* is translated from the Greek word *speiro* which means "to sow and scatter seed."[39] The word *speiro* is taken from the root word *spao* which means to "draw one's sword."[40] Therefore, when the anointed man or woman of God is sowing the Word, they are drawing their sword.

Paul says that "The sword of the Spirit . . . is the word of God" (Ephesians 6:17). And the writer of Hebrews says that the word is alive and powerful:

> For the word of God is quick, and powerful, and sharper
> than any twoedged sword, piercing even to the dividing
> asunder of soul and spirit, and of the joints and marrow,
> and is a discerner of the thoughts and intents of the heart.
> (Heb. 4:12)

It's not a two-edged sword; it's an instrument that is much sharper than a two-edged sword. The Greek word for *sharper* is *tomoteros*, which means "to cut more comprehensive or decisive as if by a single stroke."[41]

When the anointed man or woman of God is sowing the word with intent, it is like making a surgical cut. It is with precision and on purpose, and it will always bring forth fruit:

> So shall my word be that goeth forth out of my mouth: it
> shall not return unto me void, but it shall accomplish that
> which I please, and it shall prosper in the thing whereto
> I sent it. (Isa. 55:11)

The secrets and mysteries of the kingdom of God belong to those who are good ground. That ground must be prepared to receive the

39. Thayer and Smith, "Greek Lexicon entry for Speiro," The KJV New Testament Greek Lexicon, accessed November 11, 2020, https://www.biblestudytools.com/lexicons/greek/kjv/speiro.html.

40. Thayer and Smith, "Greek Lexicon entry for Spao," The KJV New Testament Greek Lexicon, accessed November 11, 2020, https://www.biblestudytools.com/lexicons/greek/kjv/spao.html.

41. Strong's Hebrew and Greek Dictionaries, s.v. "*tomoteros,*" 1890, public domain.

seed. If properly prepared, the supernatural seed that is sown will reap a supernatural harvest. The seed, the ground, and the harvest belong to the faithful servant of God.

> The secret things belong unto the LORD our God: but those things which are revealed belong unto us and to our children forever, that we may do all the words of this law. (Deut. 29:29)

> The secret of the LORD is with them that fear him; and he will shew them his covenant. (Ps. 25:14)

> The king said to the faithful servants, "Well done, good and faithful servant; thou hast been faithful over a few things, I will make thee ruler over many things: enter thou into the joy of thy Lord." (Matt. 25:21)

According to Josephus, at the time of Jesus in Israel there were about 6,000 Pharisees, 4,000 Essenes, and a few Sadducees. Each one had their own beliefs or doctrine that they believed and taught their followers. The Pharisees believed in the resurrection, and the Sadducees did not. The Essenes interpreted the Torah very strictly, and many of them separated themselves from the others and lived in Qumran and are said to have produced the Dead Sea Scrolls. They all believed that they were Israelites and the chosen people of God. They all worshiped the same God in the same temple.

I think they were very much like the Christian church today. There are many denominations with their doctrine of the Bible taught by them. They all claim to worship the same God and teach from the same Bible.

In His teaching, Jesus is trying to bring clarity to the Word of God. One example of this is in the Beatitudes where Jesus is saying, "This is what you believe, but let me show you what is the heart of the Father." For example:

> Ye have heard that it was said by them of old time, Thou
> shalt not kill; and whosoever shall kill shall be in danger
> of the judgment: But I say unto you, That whosoever
> is angry with his brother without a cause shall be in
> danger of the judgment: and whosoever shall say to
> his brother, Raca, shall be in danger of the council: but
> whosoever shall say, Thou fool, shall be in danger of hell
> fire. (Matt. 21–22)

The problem that Jesus was having in teaching in the synagogues and the temple is that you can't teach people who refuse to be taught. They refuse to hear and respond to the Word of God; therefore, He taught them through parables. When you teach through parables, only the student who is truly seeking truth will take the time to dig it out of the teaching. The true student of the Word of God will study, research, and meditate it until they receive the revelation and it comes alive in their spirit. Jesus is telling His disciples that they can't see and they can't hear, therefore they can't discern what Jesus is teaching them. He tells His disciples that these people are like the lazy servant in His parable of the "Talents." The lazy servant lost even what he thought he had, and then was cast out of the kingdom.

I am sorry to say that I think this describes much of the church today. They are willing to do their religious duty and go to church, but that is all they do. They never truly engage and commit to Jesus. They have no real interest in going deep into the Word of God. Even when you tell them that to know the Word is to know God, they still don't respond. They have eyes but don't see, and they have ears but don't hear, therefore they cannot discern the Word of God.

When we receive Jesus as our savior by being born again, we are translated into the kingdom of God. As "kingdom citizens" we are expected to conduct ourselves as a citizen, knowing the laws and customs of the kingdom. We learn that from the Word of God. The Lord gave us the "fivefold ministry" to teach and help us learn the Word (see Ephesians 4:11–13). We are expected to take advantage of that and be good students of the Word of God. Learning never stops in the kingdom of God because we can never plumb the depths of the Word. In other words, there is so much to learn that we will never learn it all in this lifetime, therefore there is never a time to stop seeking more of the Word.

Learning to sow the Word is so very important to our kingdom life. We not only need to sow the Word into our own lives, but we should be sowing into others as well. Jesus said to "make disciples, teaching them the Word of God."

I tend to want to remind the "saints" that "Judgment Day" is coming and the books will be open and we will be judged out of those books according to our works. The question then becomes, what will Jesus say to us? Will He say, "Well done thou good and faithful servant?" or will He just say, "Well, you're done"? Saying that should not be necessary. We should be so grateful for what Jesus has done for us that we are eager to learn the Word and please Him.

Everything God does, He does by a pattern based on a principle. If we don't know the principle, we can't apply it to our life. Therefore, we must get into the Word, study, and learn the principles so we can live by them, being approved by God and living a successful life in the kingdom of God. Sow the Word!

CHAPTER 11: THE PATIENCE OF JESUS CHRIST

I n the book of Revelation we find the Apostle John in his home in Ephesus dictating a letter that Jesus had commanded him to write to the seven churches which are in Asia. John's faithful servant Prochorus is writing it down as John speaks it forth, just as Jesus had spoken it to him when he was on the island of Patmos.

We should stop here and look at the context to see how John arrived in Ephesus and what is behind this letter he is writing.

John is writing this letter about AD 97, but Paul had arrived in Ephesus forty-four years earlier in AD 53 with his ministry team, Aquila and his wife, Priscilla. Paul had met this couple in Rome and they had begun to travel with Paul and help him establish churches throughout Asia. Aquila and Priscilla helped train Apollos, who Paul ordained and set in as bishop in Corinth.

Between AD 53 and AD 67, Paul and his ministry team established not only the church at Ephesus, but other churches in Asia.

In AD 67, Paul and Peter were martyred in Rome. According to traditional history, Paul was beheaded and Peter was crucified upside down on the same day at opposite ends of the city. When John learned of the death of Paul and Peter, he went to Ephesus with Mary the mother of Jesus. John was about sixty-four years old at this time.

When Prochorus, one of the seven, now the bishop of Nicodemia, heard of these events, he turned over his ministry to his associate and went to Ephesus to serve John (Acts 6:5).

In AD 93, twenty-six years after John went to Ephesus, he was arrested for refusing to worship the Emperor Domination. John was about ninety years old now.

After staying in jail in Ephesus for about two years, John was taken to Rome in AD 95 to stand trial before the Emperor Domitian, and Prochorus went with him, always by his side to take care of him.

When John came before Domitian at trial, Domitian gave him one more chance to burn incense to the Emperor and worship him, but John refused to do it.

John is thrown into a pot of boiling oil, and without being harmed, climbed out—which frightened Domitian so much that he had John exiled to the Isle of Patmos.

Prochorus, always by John's side taking care of him, voluntarily goes with him to Patmos. It was when they were on the Isle of Patmos that the Lord came to John and gave him the revelation that he was now writing to the seven churches in Asia.

In AD 96, Domitian was killed and John was pardoned. John was on Patmos for about eighteen months. John goes back to Ephesus and lived to be (according to tradition) one hundred to one hundred and four years old before he died. It is believed that all of John's writings were done at Ephesus, and Prochorus wrote them as John dictated them. Upon John's death, Prochorus went back to Nicodemia and resumed his position as bishop. Sometime later he was killed by a mob while preaching at Antioch.

CHAPTER 11: THE PATIENCE OF JESUS CHRIST

Now we are back to AD 97 and John, in obedience to Jesus, wrote to the seven churches in Asia.

> I John, who also am your brother, and companion in tribulation, and in the kingdom and patience of Jesus Christ, was in the isle that is called Patmos, for the word of God, and for the testimony of Jesus Christ. (Rev. 1:9)

This scripture is the focus of the study in this chapter. Many years ago the Holy Spirit led me to this scripture and challenged me to explain what John was saying.

He identifies himself, first, as their brother, (one who is one of them), Then he identifies himself as their companion, (a co-participant). He is saying to them, "brothers, we are participating together in; tribulation, the kingdom, and the patience of Jesus Christ."

John is locating himself. He gave his physical address, but more importantly, he gave his spiritual address. He is saying that he was in the Isle of Patmos, he is in tribulation, he is in the kingdom, he is in the patience, and he is in Jesus.

As the Holy Spirit was dealing with me about this scripture, I began to think to myself that I understand what John is saying when he said that he is their brother and companion in tribulation, but what is the "kingdom and patience of Jesus Christ?"

I know something about the kingdom of God or the kingdom of Jesus Christ, but I had never stopped to consider what was the patience of Jesus Christ. I had run into this word *patience* before in Scripture, but it usually only confused me. I especially didn't care for it in the book of James, where he says, "My brethren, count it all joy when ye fall into divers temptations; Knowing this, that the trying of your faith worketh patience. But let patience have her perfect work, that ye may be perfect and entire, wanting nothing" (James 1:2–4).

When I had read this scripture I thought to myself, "Count it all joy?" I'm thinking that I don't need patience; I need results. Misinterpreting scripture is what you get when you only read the surface of the King James Bible. What we have to do is get an understanding of the word *patience.*

John wrote this letter about AD 97. He is an old man. You would think he would be past living in tribulation by now. After all, isn't he the one who wanted to call down fire on the Samaritans? Yes, and he is also the one who had a brother with as much zeal as he and got his head chopped off.

The truth is, John is an old man. He has lived a long time. He has lived in tribulation, in the kingdom, in patience, and in Jesus for a long time. What John's life experience has taught him is that tribulation, the kingdom, patience, and Jesus all go together—it's a package deal. If we are in the kingdom of God and if we are in Jesus, tribulation will come. Jesus says that we must overcome tribulation.

Three times Jesus says, "he that hath an ear to hear what the Spirit is saying," and eight times He says, "he that overcometh." Here are just a few examples of these:

> He that hath an ear, let him hear what the Spirit saith unto the churches; To him that overcometh will I give to eat of the tree of life, which is in the midst of the paradise of God. (Rev. 2:7)

> He that hath an ear, let him hear what the Spirit saith unto the churches; He that overcometh shall not be hurt of the second death. (Rev. 2:11)

As we continue to study, we will find that the key to overcoming is patience. We also have to be able to hear what the Spirit is saying.

What is patience? The ancients called it the Queen of all virtues. Tertullian, who lived between AD 197 and AD 220, when writing about

134

"patience" started his discourse by saying that he did not believe he was worthy to even discuss the subject, much less teach on it. He went on to write quite a bit about it. The following are some quotes from his treatises:

- Patience is the "mother of mercy."

- "Let us remember that obedience itself is drawn from patience.""The art of deserving favor is obedience, while the rule of obedience is a compliant subjection.""Patience is God's nature."[42]

Let us go back to the book of James and look at these scriptures again now that we have a little more understanding of the word *patience*.

> My brethren, count it all joy when ye fall into divers temptations; Knowing this, that the trying of your faith worketh patience. But let patience have her perfect work, that ye may be perfect and entire, wanting nothing. (James 1:2-4)

This is what the Holy Spirit spoke to me about this scripture: "Let your faith perfect your patience, and your patience will perfect you."

In the passage of scripture that we are studying, the word *patience* is translated from the Greek word *hupomeno*, which means: "to *stay under* (*behind*), that is, *remain*; figuratively to *undergo*, that is, *bear* (trials), *have fortitude, persevere:* - abide, endure, (take) patient (-ly), suffer, tarry behind."[43]

Hupomeno is made up of two other Greek words, *Hupo* and *Men'-o*.

42. Quintus Tertullianus, *Of Patience*, approx.. AD 201.

43. Thayer and Smith, "Greek Lexicon entry for Hupomeno," The KJV New Testament Greek Lexicon, accessed November 11, 2020, https://www.biblestudytools.com/lexicons/greek/kjv/hupomeno.html.

Hupo *hoop-o':* A primary preposition; *under*, that is, (with the genitive) of place (*beneath*), or with verbs (the agency or means, *through*); (with the accusative) of place (whither [*underneath*] or where [*below*]) or time (when [*at*]): - among, by, from, in, of, under, with. In compounds, it retains the same genitive applications, especially of *inferior* position or condition, and specifically *covertly* or *moderately*.

men'-o: A primary verb; to *stay* (in a given place, state, relation or expectancy): - abide, continue, dwell, endure, be present, remain, stand, tarry (for), X thine own.

As you can see by the Greek definitions, the word speaks more to endurance than it does to our English translation of the word *patience*. After much study and meditation on the subject, the Holy Spirit gave me His definition of the word *patience* or *hupomeno*.

The Holy Spirit said to me that *hupomeno is having the audacity to take God at His word and the tenacity to stand in it until it manifest.*

I call it "Bulldog Tenacity." This is how Jesus overcame, and this is how we will overcome.

Jesus, operating in the earth as a man, had to do the same thing that we have to do. He had to learn the same lessons that we have to learn. Jesus humbled Himself and became obedient, even unto death (see Phil. 2:5–11, Heb. 5:8).

Jesus functioned as a man while He was on the earth. He laid down His divinity and learned to operate through developing His faith and patience. If He did it, then He expects us to do it.

God said what He meant, and He meant what He said! He said to me, "If you can change your mind, you can change your life."

Now that we know what patience is, we have to make a decision. Is the Word of God true?

136

God is not a man, that he should lie; neither the son of man, that he should repent: hath he said, and shall he not do it? or hath he spoken, and shall he not make it good? (Num. 23:19)

Is it true today? Yes! "Jesus Christ the same yesterday, and to day, and for ever" (Heb. 13:8).

Is it true for me? Yes! "Then Peter opened his mouth, and said, Of a truth I perceive that God is no respecter of persons" (Acts 10:34).

Will God back it up? Yes! "Then said the LORD unto me, Thou hast well seen: for I will hasten my word to perform it" (Jer. 1:12).

God wants to grow you up. God said it, I believe it, that settles it. Get a do-or-die attitude. Be like Shadrach, Meshach, and Abednego:

Shadrach, Meshach, and Abednego, answered and said to the king, O Nebuchadnezzar, we are not careful to answer thee in this matter. If it be so, our God whom we serve is able to deliver us from the burning fiery furnace, and he will deliver us out of thine hand, O king. But if not, be it known unto thee, O king, that we will not serve thy gods, nor worship the golden image which thou hast set up. (Dan. 3:16-18)

These three Hebrew boys had made up their minds. As far as they were concerned, the decision was final. No more discussion was necessary.

God said what He meant, and He meant what He said. He said that He will give you wisdom. This must be settled in our hearts!

Beloved, think it not strange concerning the fiery trial which is to try you, as though some strange thing happened unto you. (1 Pet. 4:12)

> Every man's work shall be made manifest: for the day shall declare it, because it shall be revealed by fire; and the fire shall try every man's work of what sort it is. (1 Cor. 3:13)

> That the trial of your faith, being much more precious than of gold that perisheth, though it be tried with fire, might be found unto praise and honor and glory at the appearing of Jesus Christ. (1 Pet. 1:7)

Brothers and Sisters, the fiery trials will come, the persecution will come and the attacks will come. If you are doing anything for the King of Glory, your natural enemy satan will attack you with a vengeance. As Jesus said in John 15:20, "If they have persecuted me, they will also persecute you." We must have this bulldog tenacity to overcome.

Perfecting patience in our lives is not just to overcome the evil in our lives, but also to ensure that we receive the good that God has for us: "For ye have need of patience, that, after ye have done the will of God, ye might receive the promise" (Heb. 10:36).

We need to pay attention to what James is telling us about this patience:

> But let him ask in faith, nothing wavering. For he that wavereth is like a wave of the sea driven with the wind and tossed. For let not that man think that he shall receive any thing of the Lord. (James 1:6–7)

Matthew Henry said, "A mind that has but one single and prevailing regard to its spiritual and eternal interest, and that keeps steady in its purposes for God, will grow wise by afflictions, will continue fervent in its devotions, and will be superior to all trials and oppositions."[44]

---

44. Matthew Henry, *Matthew Henry's Commentary on the Whole Bible*, (1708 – 1714), Public Domain.

> Wherefore seeing we also are compassed about with so
> great a cloud of witnesses, let us lay aside every weight,
> and the sin which doth so easily beset us, and let us run
> with patience the race that is set before us, Looking unto
> Jesus the author and finisher of our faith; who for the joy
> that was set before him endured the cross, despising the
> shame, and is set down at the right hand of the throne of
> God. (Heb. 12:1-2)

We must continually pursue the perfection of not only our faith, but also the perfection of patience in our life. Jude's advice is a great help in this life endeavor.

> But ye, beloved, building up yourselves on your most
> holy faith, praying in the Holy Ghost, keep yourselves in
> the love of God, looking for the mercy of our Lord Jesus
> Christ unto eternal life. (Jude 1:20-21)

Praying without ceasing, as Paul advised us to do, builds up our spirit to hear the Spirit of God, and in so doing, builds our faith. We marry the grace of faith to the grace of patience, thereby making us strong in the Spirit realm and becoming overcomers in this world.

> But that on the good ground are they, which in an honest
> and good heart, having heard the word, keep it, and bring
> forth fruit with patience. (Luke 8:15)

Many of us wonder why we lack the power of God in our lives. I believe that most of the time it is simply because we lack knowledge. We don't understand the principles that operate the kingdom of God. We have to lay a strong foundation to build in the kingdom of God.

If you lay a foundation in the natural, you have to have cement. You mix cement with sand and gravel, but unless you also mix water with it, it never hardens. Let us look at this analogy:

You have cement, sand, and gravel. Cement is the Word, sand is faith, and gravel is Jesus, the rock of our foundation. Then we need water, which is patience: "That he might sanctify and cleanse it with the washing of water by the word" (Eph. 5:26).

The cement, the sand, the gravel, and the water are all the elements you need to make a strong foundation. You have to have all of it. If you leave any part out, you have nothing.

This is where we want to be: having the audacity to take God at His Word, and the tenacity to stand in it until it manifest. Work the Word, and the Word will work.

CONCLUSION

I n the introduction we established our goal, which is to live in the "kingdom and patience of Jesus Christ." That is our set goal; that is where we want to live, and we can live there while we are still here on the earth. Jesus told us to seek first the kingdom of God and His righteousness. We enter into the kingdom of God by passing through the strait gate and narrow way. Jesus told us that only a few would be able to do that.

I trust that by now you have asked Jesus to come into your heart and be the Lord of your life. Having done that, the next step we want to take is to sit with Jesus on that couch we talked about where He shares the secrets of God with us.

To get there we need to know who we are in Christ Jesus. We should be studying the kingdom of God so we can learn not only what the kingdom is, but we can learn who we are in the kingdom. Most Christians don't have an understanding of who they are and the level of privilege that they have in the kingdom of God.

The Bible tells us that the Spirit of God will teach us the way, but we still have a responsibility to seek after knowledge. We have to put in the time to study and pray and seek first the kingdom and His righteousness. We can't be lazy; we have to study, we have to pray, we have to seek and pray in tongues. You're not going to get on that couch just by reading this book or simply desiring to sit there. Only those with passion for Jesus's presence have a chance of sitting on that couch.

The secrets of the Lord are only for those who "fear" him. That speaks of high reverential respect, the respect that only comes from someone who passionately loves the object of their desire. The kind of passion that sets everything else aside to focus entirely on the object of their desire. They will not allow anything to come between them and the object of their desire.

When Jesus becomes your passion and the object of your desire, then and only then is there any chance of being invited to that couch. Jesus desires that you sit on that couch with Him much more than you do, but you have to do your part—and it's not an easy goal to achieve! You can get there; He is patiently waiting for you to be willing to give up this world and decide that He is the only priority in your life.

The secret of the Lord is that which cannot be known unless the Lord reveals it.

There are things that the Lord desires to reveal to you that you will never know just by reading the Bible and going to church. You can hear every great preacher and read all their books but the secrets of the Lord are only for those who sit on that couch. That's why I want to sit on that couch with Him. The more of the Word that I know, the more I know Him. He is all wise, He is all-knowing, He is all understanding. To know the Word is to know Jesus. My passion for Him is inexhaustible—I can't get enough. The one thing that I have learned in all of my studies and all of my learning and all of my seeking, is that the more I learn, the more I realize how little I know. You can never plumb the depths of God, there is always more.

He also said that if you can qualify to sit on that couch, He will show you His covenant. That simply means He will demonstrate His Word to you. All the rights, privileges, and benefits of the covenant will be laid before you as a banquet feast for your desire. I believe that this is God's will for you and me. We can not only sit in Jesus at the right hand of God in heavenly places, but we can sit on this couch with Jesus, receiving impartations and anointings, but above all, just being in a very special place in Him.

Covenant Language

As I said before, the first obstacle that must be overcome in any study of the Word of God is to understand that the Bible was written by Eastern people, to Eastern people, in Eastern language. We cannot translate Eastern language that is thousands of years old to our twenty-first century Western, English language and expect to retain the full meaning of the idea behind the word being translated. Therefore, if we want to know more about what is being said, we have to dig deeper than Strong's or Thayer's.

You should now be familiar with the language of the covenant that was used or expressed in ancient history. When you understand the language of covenant expressed in writings or conversation in ancient times, you can then identify in the Bible when it is speaking of the covenant. When you can recognize ancient rites and customs when referring to making a covenant, then you have a more clear picture of the subject being discussed. When people in ancient times wrote to each other, they assumed the person they were writing to understood what they were saying without the need to give detailed information on the subject. We, however, don't know what they are saying, so we will read right past it and never know the weight of the subject being discussed.

I highly recommend that you continue to study the ancient rites, customs, and practices of blood covenant peoples.

In the English language, the word *covenant* speaks about two parties joining together in a way that cannot be broken, like any other agreement. In the Bible the word *covenant* is meant in this strong manner, which is essential to understand when we are talking about covenants.

When the student can recognize and understand covenant language they will be able to interpret the Word of God to a greater level of revelation in what is being discussed. The student will then be able to see covenant language throughout the Old and the New Testament, thereby opening levels of understanding which would before not been available to the student without this knowledge.

The Word of God is filled with knowledge, but for the student to be able to receive that knowledge they must be knowledgeable themselves of ancient customs, rites, and practices.

Primitive Covenant

Earlier in the book we looked at the actual process of making a covenant. There are elements of making a covenant that is necessary for all forms of the blood covenant. For instance, all blood covenants involve the shedding of blood by the partners making the covenant, whether it is their blood or the blood of a substitute. The substitute can be a person or it can be an animal. All blood covenants have a blessings clause and a curse clause. All blood covenants will establish a memorial to ensure the remembrance of the covenant, thereby causing all partners in the covenant to honor the covenant.

All of these elements of blood covenant are found in the covenants God made with man. We study these covenant rites and practices so we can understand the sacredness of the covenant we have with Almighty God. We must know that we are covenant people and are responsible before God to uphold our part in the covenant we have with God.

The purpose of a covenant is to establish a relationship that is impossible to break. The covenant has procedures and customs which guarantee the relationship. It has both a curse to discourage breaking the relationship, and blessing to encourage loyalty. In God's covenant, His motivation for keeping His Word is His love, not the fear of a curse.

God is loyal and faithful, even when we are not. Human love without a covenant always has a self-preservation and self-protection quality about it. Human love is never totally unselfish apart from a covenant. It can never completely give of itself for fear of being hurt. But God's love gives and gives—even when nothing is given in return.

Threshold Covenant

It would seem that the threshold covenant was the most common covenant practiced in the Eastern world. The practice was found throughout the world. It was held to be a most sacred covenant.

Some scholars believe that the Passover in Egypt was a threshold covenant with God. I too believe that it was a threshold covenant. All the elements of a threshold covenant are displayed on that night. The sacrifice, the blood on the doorpost, and the angel passing over the blood.

I also believe that God was showing that He is a personal God in requiring each house to participate in the covenant. If He wanted to just cover His people corporately He could have required the elders to do the sacrifice at the city gates. He said, "A lamb for a house." I believe that shows that God made a personal covenant with each family. We should also notice that there was no explanation as to what He required to do this covenant. These people were already familiar with the threshold covenant and recognized what God was doing. The Father of the house knew exactly what to do.

The blessings of the covenant were also displayed when they left Egypt. In Exodus, we see that they left with the riches of Egypt:

> And the children of Israel did according to the word of Moses; and they borrowed of the Egyptians jewels of silver, and jewels of gold, and raiment: And the LORD gave the people favour in the sight of the Egyptians, so that they lent unto them such things as they required. And they spoiled the Egyptians. (Ex. 12:35–36)

When He made a covenant with the Hebrews, not only did he make them rich—He also healed all their diseases: "He brought them forth also with silver and gold: and there was not one feeble person among their tribes" (Psalm 105:37). The curse of the covenant was also displayed as they wandered in the wilderness for the next forty years when they disobeyed God.

Obviously, Jesus was aware of threshold covenants. He referred to the threshold covenant in John 10:1–2:

> Verily, verily, I say unto you, He that entereth not by the door into the sheepfold, but climbeth up some other way, the same is a thief and a robber. But he that entereth in by the door is the shepherd of the sheep.

Apparently, the knowledge and practice of the threshold covenant were quite common in their culture. The student should now be able to recognize a threshold covenant as you study the Word of God.

Salt Covenant

As we found in our study of the salt covenant, it is almost the same as a blood covenant. It is a substitute for blood. When blood is not available, salt can be used, and it holds as much power and is just as scared as the blood.

When you share salt with a person, you come into covenant with that person. The difference is depending on the culture at the time. It may be a permanent covenant or it may be a temporary covenant. It contains the blessings and the curses of the covenant. The ancient Rabbis said that the reason God destroyed Sodom was that they violated the covenant of salt. God also required that salt be included in the burnt offerings in the temple. The Bible says that God gave the throne to David and his descendants by the covenant of salt. Therefore, we find that the covenant of salt was just as sacred and powerful as the traditional blood covenant or the threshold covenant.

Hesed

God's lovingkindness is never-ending and never weakening. The object of His love is always at the forefront of His mind. Of course, the object of His love is you! It doesn't matter how unworthy you may feel, He is always thinking about you. He is always working His plan to make you more compatible with the kingdom of God. That's where He wants you to be so He can shower you with all His wonderful blessings. The greater you are assimilated into the kingdom of God, the greater He can bless you.

God's *hesed* toward you is so great that it cannot be explained. We mortals cannot grasp the weight of His love. He tells us, "For my thoughts are not your thoughts, neither are your ways my ways…For as the heavens are higher than the earth, so are my ways higher than your ways, and my thoughts than your thoughts" (Isa. 55:8–9).

God's *hesed* is irrevocable, it cannot be altered in any way. It is irrevocably tied to covenant and truth. The three cannot be separated. Just as God the Father, God the Son, and God the Holy Spirit cannot be separated, neither can covenant, *hesed*, and truth be separated. They are one. There is no covenant without them. We must meditate this principle until it comes alive in our spirit. This principle in the kingdom of God is so powerful that when the revelation comes, we become powerful in the realm of the Spirit.

When *hesed* is connected to covenant it is never-ending. It is passed down to the next generation. A good example of this is when David and Jonathan made a covenant. Some twenty years after Jonathan had died, David could not rest until he had found someone in Jonathan's family he could bless (see 2 Sam. 9:1).

David brought Jonathan's son to his house and he sat at the king's table all of his life. We, too, are in covenant with a King. He has invited us to come and dine with Him.

We should start believing the Word of God and begin to receive the blessings of the covenant we have with Almighty God. His *hesed* is new every morning. His lovingkindness endures forever. He is standing at the door and knocking, waiting for you to invite Him to step over the blood on the door sill and come in and partake of the covenant meal with you.

Behold, I stand at the door, and knock: if any man hear my voice, and open the door, I will come in to him, and will sup with him, and he with me. (Rev. 3:20)

Genesis 1:1 says that "in the beginning God created." John 1:1 says that "in the beginning was the Word" and "all things were made by Him." And the Word became flesh and was our blood sacrifice taking us into covenant with Almighty God. He created and then He provided everything necessary for a life in Him in the kingdom of God.

The realms that are beyond the gate are there for our benefit and enjoyment, but we must learn how to access the principles that govern the kingdom of God. Remember that everything God does is according to a pattern and based on a principle. We can learn those principles, and thereby work the pattern entering into the kingdom of God and accessing all the rights, privileges, and benefits that are provided in the covenant we have with Almighty God.

In the study of these principles, I pray that you have been enlightened and are thereby strengthened in faith. All of these principles that we have studied are very powerful and should make your walk in the kingdom more rewarding and fulfilling. Jesus said that the Holy Spirit will lead you into all truth and I believe if you ask Him, He will take you further into His realms than even this study will take you. There is always more to be revealed; no one person knows it all. The Holy Spirit delights in leading the passionate seeker into greater revelation. He will not disappoint; He will lead you higher and higher into His realm.

A true blood covenant with Almighty God must include *hesed* and truth. It cannot be a true covenant without them. They cannot be separated from a covenant. These three elements of the covenant are the very foundation, even the very lifeblood of our relationship with an Almighty God. As you have studied the realms of the kingdom of God, you should have noticed that each one is tied directly to covenant. Each principle comes out of covenant. The principles of salvation, imputed righteousness, baptism in the Holy Spirit, sowing and reaping, and patience cannot be without the covenant. It amazes me that we, as faithful students of the Bible, spend so much time studying everything but the covenant. We spend so little time on the subject that we have a very little revelation of our covenant privileges. All of the kingdom principles are very important to our kingdom experience, but we must realize that without the covenant—and especially the revelation of the covenant—we will never experience the power that is available through the activation of these principles. These principles will never be activated in our life without taking the time to study and mediate these principles until they come alive in our spirit.

The knowledge you have gained in reading this book is certainly not all there is to know about these subjects. I desire that you take what you have learned and build on it. The Holy Spirit will lead you into all truth if you will zealously seek it. We will never plumb the depths of the Word of God, there is always more to be learned. We should let Paul's advice to Timothy be our standard so that at His coming we will not be ashamed.

> Study to shew thyself approved unto God, a workman that needeth not to be ashamed, rightly dividing the word of truth. (2 Tim. 2:15)

ABOUT THE AUTHOR

D r. Bill Means has been in the ministry for over twenty years. He and his wife established and pastored a non-denominational church in Fort Smith, Arkansas, for over fourteen years. He is the president of Inner Circle Ministries, which focuses on building people, raising them up, and sending them out into ministry. He received his Doctorate from St. Thomas Christian University in Jacksonville, Florida, in April of 2019. Dr. Means ministers in Africa and South America, as well as in the United States of America. For more information: www.innercircleministries.org.

CPSIA information can be obtained
at www.ICGtesting.com
Printed in the USA
FSHW021031240621
82609FS